AWAKENING TO 'I AM LOVE'

AWAKENING TO 'I AM LOVE'

HOW FINDING YOUR TRUE SELF TRANSFORMS YOUR WELLBEING, RELATIONSHIPS, AND WHAT YOU DO

DAVID YOUNGREN

Copyright @ 2019 by David Youngren

All rights reserved.

Published in the United States by Anora Press

No part of this book may be reproduced in any form or by any electronic or mechanical means, including information storage and retrieval systems, without written permission from the author, except for the use of brief quotations in a book review.

This edition of the book was updated and modified in 2020 from its original edition.

CONTENTS

Preface   vii
Introduction   xi

PART I
THE PRIMARY QUESTIONS OF LIFE

1. The Search for Freedom   3
2. What Is Love?   16
3. Stages of Consciousness   32

PART II
THE FALSE SELF

4. The Formation of the Ego   47
5. The Illusion of Good and Evil   57
6. The Quest of the Ego   73
7. The Myth of Failure   85

PART III
THE AWAKENING

8. The Wonder of Who You Are   99
9. The Unfolding Creation   109
10. The Heart Transformation   122
11. When Faith Reveals Who You Are   131
12. How Meditation Helps You Awaken   146

PART IV
THE MANIFESTATION OF YOUR TRUE SELF

13. A Mindset of Love   161
14. A Better World   174

References and Recommendations   187
Notes   191
About David Youngren   193

PREFACE

The phrase *I am Love* can be both empowering and confusing. The words *I* and *am* identify who we are, which is inspiring, and gratifying. And no word is as mesmerizing, affectionate, and warm as *love*.

Yet to begin with *I am,* and then finish with *love* just doesn't seem right. A more acceptable expression is either *I am Loved* or *Love Yourself*. But as we will explore in this book, love is more than something you do to yourself when you are struggling, or experience when you look at your gorgeous wife or hunk of a boyfriend, or feel when you hold your baby in your arms. Love is the essence of who you are. It's your *true self*.

And that matters because waking up to *love* within you not only transforms what you do; it transforms the way you live. It will improve your emotional, physical, mental, and spiritual wellbeing, and enrich your relationships with your partner, family, friends, neighbors, and co-workers. In fact, awakening to love within us is our shared path to a more peaceful, compassionate, and equitable new earth.

But I get it. It's strange to define yourself as love (don't try it at your next job interview). It's much easier to create a label based on where you come from, your first name, your last name, your status, your career, your title(s), your hobbies, your income, your looks, your achievements, your education, your race, your sexuality, your gender, your nationality, your religion, your political affiliation, your family, your marital status, your age, and where you live.

In addition to the way these identity markers color our perceptions of ourselves, we have also been shaped by our experiences, traumas, and the beliefs of others. Somehow all of these ideas and inputs have been scrambled together in our subconscious and formed our sense of self.

The problem is that these unconscious concepts about our identity have left us wounded and fearful. That fear has entrenched itself in our thoughts, and has even been wired into our biological neural networks. Lost in the illusions of the mind, we have forgotten the essence of our being. We are like Sleeping Beauty: unconscious of who we are.

Through behavior modification, religious piety, and a lot of therapy sessions, we have tried to hide, ignore, or forget the fearful thoughts that produced our insecurities, shame, and guilt. But fear is intrusive and prevailing. It's been impossible to silence.

It sabotages our careers, ends our relationships, and infects our children. It makes us obsess and overeat, hide and attack, drink and do drugs, control and ignore—anything to escape, if only for a moment, the nagging feeling that we are not enough the way we are.

Our behavior and actions stem from how we view ourselves. We act out who we believe ourselves to be. When fear hijacks the way we see ourselves, we feel less worthy. To cope with this inner confusion and chaos, we create a *false self* that we assume will restore our worth and value. This false self craves validation; it pines for acceptance and approval and dons a variety of masks to get it.

Each person's masks are different, but they all serve the same purpose: to acquire love from an external source. We all want to be loved—first by our parents, then, if that fails, by our peers. We have lost touch with the dimension within us that is love, so we compensate by doing whatever we have to do to gain acceptance and love from the outside.

The less conscious we are of unconditional love already within us, the more dysfunctional we become. Darkness blankets our consciousness, and we respond with anger, anxiety, depression, obsession, bitterness, addiction, hatred, withdrawal, and jealousy. Fear itself becomes our private hell, and amidst our suffering, our minds demand some form of revenge. That is when we turn our fear outward and create hell for others through manipulation, control, abuse, greed, violence, murder, and even war.

This is why we must move past the fearful thinking that surrounds our *true self*, and awaken to the love that we are. Conscious of an inward witness of *I AM LOVE* is the seed that bears the fruits of happiness, peace, compassion, kindness, and goodness in our lives.

INTRODUCTION
THE STORY BEHIND THIS BOOK

A year before I was born in Sweden, my sister Elisabeth was playing in a pool of rainwater that had filled the foundation of a construction site near our family's home. Tragically, she drowned that day, ending her short life. According to my parents, she was an adorable little girl who was graced with exceptional beauty and charm, and who had everyone she met completely smitten. Full of potential and life, my parents had big hopes for her. I can only imagine the pain and guilt they must have faced with her loss.

Maybe my conception was a welcome relief to the pain they felt. Or perhaps I was an unconscious replacement for the girl they loved so much. I asked my mother about it many years later—*Was I a replacement for Elisabeth?*—but she never gave me a straightforward answer. Looking back on it, who could blame her?

Nevertheless, on a deeper level, my perception that I was a replacement for Elisabeth had a significant impact on me and contributed to my learning fear. To my young mind, hearing about my sister's unique charm and beauty only reinforced that I was not like her. I was somehow less than her, and maybe even a disappointment of some sort. The sentiment running through the back of my mind was: *I'm not enough the way I am.*

My intention, of course, is not to cast blame on my parents. Fear is a virus that has been passed down to all of us, and we in turn unintentionally pass it down to our children. I was, for the most part, raised in a wonderful and loving family, but even in the most idyllic of childhoods we can't escape from the intrusiveness of fear.

Searching for Love

We all come into this world like a sponge absorbing everything around us. Along the way, we develop our identity—derived mainly from our parents or the primary caretakers in our early life. Seeking to identify with the person(s) whose love we crave the most, we often become what we subconsciously perceive they want us to be in the hope that we will be loved, accepted, and approved by them.

If the ones whose love we craved were always struggling financially, that might lead us to focus on making money. We instinctively feel, "If I can make enough money, maybe I will get the approval that I desire." For others, their craving for love may lead them to a specific art form, a particular type of education or career, a hobby, sports, or the ministry, all because intuitively they believe these pursuits will give them the love and acceptance that they seek.

As far back as I can remember, I felt "the call" into a world-wide ministry. My mother had always dreamed of preaching globally. When she was young, she traveled from church to church in Sweden until she met my dad in her early twenties. By the time she was in her mid-twenties, she was married and had a child. Her dream had to take a backseat to her family.

Years later when I was a teenager, my older brother, Peter, moved to Canada and became a well-known international evangelist. When I observed my parents' pride in Peter's achievements, that desire in me to be a minister only intensified (perhaps accentuated in part by my longing to earn the same acceptance they gave my brother). I was looking for unconditional love, because lodged deep inside my heart was the fear that I was not enough the way I was. Serving in the ministry seemed like a sure way to get my parents approval.

Keep in mind that none of this occurred to me as a conscious thought at the time. But subconsciously the need for love and acceptance were guiding my pursuits. Looking back, I can see how many of my decisions in my life were influenced by my insecurities. Nothing really escaped this torrent of uneasiness and apprehension during my first forty years.

By that time, I was the Pastor of a church just outside of Toronto, the President of a Ministerial College, and I travelled the world speaking in large city-wide crusades. I even had my own television show! But none of it was enough to acquire the love I felt I had to earn.

Although I enjoyed my success, I still struggled with insecurity, worry, and depression. I was never truly happy because I was seeking from outside sources something that was already inside of me.

I remember many phone calls with my mom when I was eager to tell her about my success, only to have her innocently turn the conversation to her own ministry, or the success of my siblings. After my discussions with her, I often felt quite irritable. I didn't know why those conversations brought up those emotions in me at the time, but looking back on it now it seems clear: the answer to the question *Am I enough for love?* would have been just too painful to explore.

A mindset of fear is a destructive force. It destroys us from within. It is the underlying cause of the dysfunctions, the instability, and the suffering we experience. Unaware of unconditional love because fear has intruded, we know no other way than to self-aggrandize, self-sabotage, and self-punish.

How Awareness of Unconditional Love Changed Me

In 2005, a unique series of events led to me leaving the success I had built in Canada. Career-wise it felt like I was on the top of my game. Simmering below the surface, however, was a broken human being. The subtext of my life until that point was *I'm not enough as I am*. As a result, I had worn many different masks throughout my life, dysfunctional and self-righteous alike, all of which my ego believed would validate me and give me the kind of approval my heart craved.

I needed a change. We sold our home in Toronto, rented a big truck, got our minister's visa, and drove all of our belongings to San Diego, California.

Arriving in beautiful California felt like an escape at first. With two other families joining us, we thought we had hit the jackpot. But it didn't last long. How could it? I could run, but I couldn't escape myself.

In a way, settling in California only magnified my inner struggles. At least in Canada, I was busy building my career. I could hide in the adrenalin rush of success (or *the anointing* as we called it) of speaking numerous times a week. In my mind, the lows of being alone with my nagging and destructive inner dialogue were part of being a normal human. Because I got to enjoy the highs of being validated by the crowds, the lows seemed more tolerable.

But in California the highs were much less frequent. I didn't have the crowds (or at least I had a lot less of them). So I subconsciously sought validation through such experiences that would enhance my sense of self and silence the nagging doubt that I was not enough the way I was.

Of course, all of these pursuits only strengthened my fear. With a combination of intense guilt, anger, and self-righteousness, I suddenly began experiencing excruciating cluster headaches to the point where I felt like someone was sticking a knife in my eye.

No matter what I did, including seeking help from doctors and pleading with God to take the pain away, the agony only increased. Even prescription-strength painkillers could not alleviate the intense throbbing. I felt hopeless and ready to give up. Although my sermons were bathed in grace, my heart was not. So subconsciously, I internalized the pain as some sort of punishment for my failure at the hand of a disappointed God.

Then one day in 2006, I had an unexplainable deep inner prompting to close my eyes and meditate on divine love. It was completely outside of my comfort zone, but right there in my car I closed my eyes and re-lived a scene from the movie *The Passion of the Christ*. The story of Christ's death communicated the profundity of selfless and unconditional love.

Suddenly my imagination turned intimate, and for a moment I felt like I was there, immediately, in the presence of Christ while he carried his cross.

Indescribable love rushed over me.

Within mere moments, the pain subsided. Since then, I have never had another attack of cluster headaches.

From Religious to Spiritual

Strangely enough, this experience did not make me more religious. If anything, it made me less enamored with my religious tradition. It felt like my religion had misrepresented God.

A set of beliefs about God were handed down over centuries, and without much questioning or careful consideration on my part, I had simply accepted this dogma as fact. However, fear, not love, was the driving motivator behind my religion, and that fear had kept me in my religion's fold.

Following the dramatic meditation event, the way I perceived and experienced reality changed. My eyes opened in an entirely new way to the power of love. I found that this recurring message of love that transcends all else was present in many ancient sacred texts.

With a new understanding of these revered spiritual writings, my life changed. I saw God, the Universe, the Spirit, a Higher Power, the Ground of Being, the Divine Mind, the Source, or whatever name you prefer to use to describe that which transcends all through a new lens: love. I began to meditate on this pure love every day.

Love can feel vague and abstract, so in the beginning I incorporated Jesus into my meditation. Since I was raised in the Christian tradition, Jesus personified love to me. I could identify with him. The story of his death and resurrection communicated both the purity and power of love. So I kept directing my emotions and my imagination on the pure love in Jesus until my wandering thoughts came to an end. Once my thoughts ceased in my meditations, I experienced an awareness of transcending life unlike anything I had ever known or felt before. I became conscious of indescribable, pure, and selfless love.

I was not separate from the *infinite*. My mind, driven by fear, had hidden from the transcending *presence* of the universe. But God, whose essence is the force of love in the universe, surrounded me, embraced me, and flowed through me.

It was my mind that had alienated itself from the awareness of love. The evil and the selfishness that plague humanity were evidence of that fearful mind. However, fear is only an illusion of separation in the mind. The ultimate reality is the oneness of the universe—the divine unifying love that transcends all and gives life.

When the eyes of my heart were opened to this reality, my health suddenly improved drastically. My old crippling attitudes disappeared. My insecurities and fears began to fade. I found paradise within. I came to know that my true identity is love. In fact, love is who all of us are. The design of the *source* of all has been coded into our DNA. It's our true hidden self that, when awakened, will transform us both individually and collectively.

This Book Is About You

Your life path and your story are different from mine. Whatever journey you've taken so far has been important, significant, and uniquely yours. Although we may not share the same beliefs and values, we share a common humanity, which cries out for unconditional love. Intuitively we know that the greatest of all is love, and that love transforms us from the inside out.

So this book is about you—who you are and how you can practically awaken to your *true self*. Pulling from scientific discoveries, various ancient and modern texts, and the intuitive knowledge that all of us possess, I will share what I know and have experienced (all while being honest about my own limited understanding). Since my background is Christian, I will pull more from that tradition than any other. Yet my goal is not to engender a religious tribalism with this book, because I have come to realize that throughout history, the transcending *source* of all has been revealing the nature of life to people throughout the earth, regardless of religion. The concept of God is too big to be limited to only one tradition's stories (after all, who am I to discount the validity of another faith?).

This book, therefore, is not written to introduce you to a set of mental ideas and beliefs, but instead to guide you in finding your *true self*. Whether you agree with everything is irrelevant—at least to me. What matters more is that you find your *true self*, because you deserve happiness, freedom, and a life of purpose.

I'm convinced that love is the answer to your wounds, your pain, and our collective divisions. So let's explore together how you can awaken to your *true self* and rewrite the story of your human experience. Your best life awaits you!

PART I

THE PRIMARY QUESTIONS OF LIFE

Take risks. Ask big questions.

— David Packard

1
THE SEARCH FOR FREEDOM

There's something magical about the word *freedom*. Democracies are built on it, advertisers love it, and our teenage children insist on it. To live free is the dream of the bullied, troubled, upset, anxious, and suffering. It's the hope of every living being. When I think of freedom, my mind drifts to a children's tale about a colorless tiger held captive in a zoo...

The tiger's body was covered with shades of black, white, and gray. Since the tiger's fur lacked the beauty and sparkle of bright colors, it inspired a nickname among the zoo's patrons: the colorless tiger. In fact, its lack of colors brought it much fame, and painters from around the world traveled to the zoo to put color on its fur. After each painter added new colors to the colorless tiger's fur, the tiger's body took on a new (albeit brief) beauty. However, the paint never remained, always falling off its fur within days.

Then one day a crazy painter named Van Cough (not to be confused with van Gogh) came along. He was a peculiar fellow, for although he used a brush, he never used any paint or paper. He just moved his brush around in the air, seeming to *wish* his way to a painting. As you can imagine, when he arrived at the zoo to put some color on the colorless tiger, everyone laughed. Undeterred, Van Cough entered the cage and gently whispered in the tiger's ear. He then moved his brush up and down in the air while continuing to speak softly to the tiger. Suddenly, the tiger's black, white, and gray body took on dazzling new hues—the most vivid and beautiful colors a tiger ever had. Everyone was surprised and wanted to know the painter's secret. Van Cough told them that his brush could only paint real life and therefore needed no colors. Instead of paint, he had merely whispered into the tiger's ear:

In just a few days, you will be free.

Seeing how sad the tiger had been in its captivity, and how the prospect of freedom had brightened its day, the zookeepers took the tiger to the jungle where it would never again lose its color.

While most of us are not surrounded by an inescapable cage, many of us find ourselves trapped in our heads, held hostage to negative and even toxic thoughts. We are not free. To make matters worse, we don't even realize that we are not free. Even if we do know that we are not free, we don't know *how* to be free. So, like the colorless tiger, we are not reflecting our *true self*. We only show the world the drabness of our black, white, and gray fur.

We look for the right relationships to feel secure; more money to feel successful; and status, power, or fame to feel significant. We want happiness. We want our lives to matter. We want to be loved and to love without restraints. But hiding behind our pursuits is a desire for freedom from the nagging doubts, fears, and feelings that *I'm not enough the way I am.*

Of course good relationships, more money, being well-known, or having a lot of influence are all valid and worthwhile pursuits.

Good relationships are essential for wellbeing. Money is a necessary tool for living. Influence and notoriety will often come when your gifts and talents are unleashed. But finding meaning in your existence doesn't *begin* with those desires. When birthed in anything less than unconditional love, these aspirations put you in a cage because what your soul really seeks is freedom.

Freedom is the state of being where you are neither imprisoned nor enslaved. It's the absence of being dominated by anything foreign to your *true self*. When you are free, you are in a state of innocence. You are emotionally and spiritually naked, yet you are without shame. Nothing is hidden, yet you are not afraid.

We often reference freedom as the power or right to act, speak, or think as we want to without hindrance and restraints. While such liberty is the hallmark of every democratic society, it pales in significance to the mental, emotional, and spiritual freedom from fear.

When your inner being is free, fear no longer holds you captive. Anxiety, worry, doubt, apprehension, panic, unease, jealousy, and all other emotions connected to fear are no longer the controlling factors in your life. You are free from everything that stands in the way of love, happiness, peace, and meaning in life.

What's Missing When We Are Not Free

For any genuine seeker, the question of whether our spirituality brings us freedom is embryonic. What good is our spirituality if it doesn't improve our lives and the world as a whole?

Imagine for a moment that you have no spiritual, religious, or agnostic biases or beliefs. One day you are placed in a room full of people from every religious and spiritual tradition, including atheists and agnostics. Some of the people appear to be rigid, fearful, and even depressed. Others come across as unkind and bitter. But there is a group of them who are truly at peace, radiating love and compassion to everyone in the room. They have what you might call the sparkle of life. Who would you want to be around—the rigid and fearful group, or the loving and compassionate group? And whose spiritual path would you trust to work best for you?

You would probably pay little attention to what each group believed at first, instead choosing to associate with the latter group because they seemed so happy and alive. In other words, you would evaluate the authenticity of what they believed based on their level of freedom.

When I found myself in a spiritual crisis, shortly after I moved to California, I had to be willing to admit to myself that I was not free. I had influence among my peers around the world. I was a success in my field (as my many titles would attest to), and I had the money I needed for comfort, but inside I was not free. I was hostage to a plethora of negative and often subconscious thoughts that would fluctuate between self-importance, self-grandeur, and self-loathing. Beneath it all were subconscious doubts about my worth.

Plunging further into my despair, I was reminded of something Jesus said: *You shall know the truth, and the truth will make you free.* If Jesus was correct, and truth would make me free, I wanted to know what the truth was. My immediate thought was, "I have spent my entire life sharing my faith around the world, and people have validated me for that. Therefore, what I already believe must be the truth."

Yet I was faced with a troubling conundrum. If I'm not free, then I must be missing something about the essence of truth. I believed I had found the truth that makes one free, but my inner struggles and pain demonstrated an opposing reality. So right there in my misery, I silently prayed something like this to God:

"If you are real, then show me the truth, because I want to be free. No matter where it takes me, I want to know the truth more than anything else."

Immediately I felt a peace rush over me. I was opening my heart to whatever would give me the freedom that I desired. But it didn't take long for fear to interrupt my peace. Words that I had heard and used in my attempts to help people all my life came rushing back.

Don't question what you believe.

Don't open yourself to wrong ideas.

Be careful that you don't turn away.

For a moment I found myself paralyzed in my fear. Was I about to miss the truth?

Looking back I recognize how religious systems bend toward self-preservation, and how my thoughts in that moment were shaped by a system that requires conformity to survive. When we step out of line and question the system, like I was about to in that questioning moment, we will invariably get shamed and ostracized. The system may not always be wrong, but the fear and insecurity it creates in us holds us hostage to it. As a result, we are not free.

As I continued to think about being a seeker of the truth, I was reminded of how Jesus stated that a good father (God) gives good gifts to his children when we simply ask—even more so than our earthly parents. I knew I had asked for a good gift, and felt assured that I was on the right path. My heart desired freedom, and knowing the truth would get me there.

Many Want to Be Free, but Few Want the Truth

If you've ever watched the movie *A Few Good Men*, you'll probably remember the courtroom drama between the fierce General Jessup (played by Jack Nicholson) and the lazy lieutenant and defense lawyer Kaffee (played by Tom Cruise). In a heated exchange, Kaffee demands to know the truth. After a slight pause and with a furious look on his face, Jack Nicholson's character forcefully shouts back, "You can't handle the truth!"

Research now indicates that the General's angered response is more than just good acting. Most people can't handle the truth, nor do they really want to know the truth. Our minds are made up: we already know the truth (or at least that's what we've convinced ourselves).

To risk being wrong about what we believe invokes fear and insecurity. Since our sense of identity is attached to what we think, questioning our beliefs shakes the very foundation of who we are.

It is, therefore, easier to just assume that whatever we believe must be the truth. So rather than objectively pursue truth, we look for information that supports what we already think to be true. In cognitive science, this is referred to as *motivated reasoning*.

Peter Ditto, Ph.D, a social psychologist at the University of California, Irvine, who studies how motivation, emotion, and intuition influence judgment, says:

> "People are capable of being thoughtful and rational, but our wishes, hopes, fears, and motivations often tip the scales to make us more likely to accept something as true if it supports what we want to believe."[1]

In other words, our view of reality is filtered by what our minds have been conditioned to see.

We don't have to move further than our social media posts to find proof of *motivated reasoning*. We are quick to share a link if it supports our religious or political beliefs, but either ignore the story or rigorously fact-check it if it doesn't.

What's really fascinating is how our group identity affects how we (and I use the word *we* here to describe humanity as a whole) interpret facts. When we identify with a particular group, such as a nation, race, political party, religion, educational or professional group, sports team, or even a gang, the social incentives for a unified group-think are so powerful that even the most educated are unable to filter facts through an unbiased lens. We are at a deep level afraid to lose our collective identity especially when our personal lives don't add up, because at least our community provides us with a feeling of superiority and specialness. So we unconsciously alter or twist facts so as not to lose the perception that at least our tribe is exceptional (even if I'm not).

Evidence of our propensity toward group identification can be seen in all aspects of life. Professor Ditto uses the example of the current state of politics when he states that:

> "We now live in a world where there are red facts and blue facts, and I believe these biased motivated-reasoning processes fuel political conflict. If someone firmly believes some fact to be true that you just as firmly believe to be false, it is hard for either of you not to see that other person as stupid, disingenuous, or both."[2]

Religion and spirituality are no different. In my religious background, I remember seeking out texts that supported my central spiritual worldview and the group I identified with. I was not really seeking the truth as much as I was looking for evidence that would strengthen what I already considered to be the truth. Subconsciously I was driven to establish my worth so that I could feel special, and therefore get the recognition and respect that would silence the nagging doubts that *I'm not enough the way I am*. I needed to be validated within my tribe to alleviate some of the fears and insecurities that were lodged in my heart. But I was not aware that this was my motive; my mind was not yet able to consider that what I believed could be wrong.

This inability to unbiasedly seek out the truth often impacts us in ways that have enormous consequences on how we live. Think about how many people are willing to go to war for their country, or leave family and friends to go on a life-long mission in defense of their tradition. Since early childhood, we are programmed to accept the narrative of our community. So we never question it. We just assume it's true.

We have become so entrenched in our fear-induced ethnocentricity that when we struggle or experience failure, we shift responsibility to another group, political entity, race, religion, or nation. Marketing experts affirm our infinity with this kind of ethnocentricity when they propose that the key to growing a following is creating a narrative of "Us vs. Them." Their advice is simple: Throw rocks at your group's enemy, and you will get people to follow you. Nothing bonds people together like having a common enemy.

Of course, the reason why we are susceptible to this type of mass manipulation is two-fold: The *false self* needs to identify with a group that it considers unique and superior to enhance its sense of self.

And the *false self* wants justification for its failure. We blame our struggles on another group because the *false self* is convinced that finding someone else to blame will alleviate, or at least repress, our feelings of not being enough the way we are. So we seek out only the facts that support our current worldview, and categorize the rest as lies.

The inability to discern facts from lies has now become more pronounced with the emergence of social media. Hoaxes, conspiracy theories, and disinformation disguised as news are now readily available. Since this bombardment of information is right there in front of us on our device, and we can use it to support our worldview and shift blame for our troubles onto a group that we oppose, then it must be the truth. On the other hand, whatever opposes our worldview must be "fake news."

So what conclusion can we come to other than: fear has so deeply lodged itself in our minds that it's easier to twist, ignore, and alter facts, than to accept the possibility of being wrong? We are, therefore, really not seekers of truth (no wonder we struggle). The fear and insecurity that control the way we perceive reality have convinced us that it's better to protect what we believe and attack what opposes our convictions, than to search for freedom by exploring the question: what is the truth?

Knowing Truth That Makes Us Free

It's no wonder then that knowing the truth that makes us free is more complicated than we first thought. Our minds were conditioned in childhood by emotional and traumatic experiences that activated fear. This fear prevents us from seeing clearly. It has us wired to view things not as they are, but as the fear and insecurity in our minds wants and needs things to be.

So if our sense of self is rooted in a specific set of beliefs, then we are incapable of considering another path to be true. Fear keeps us in the fold. We would rather live with the familiarity of emotional pain and dysfunction, than to seek for truth. Therefore, our beliefs are holding us hostage to fear. So the very thing that we thought would make us free has now become that which makes us miss the mark, because fear is the unconscious filter through which we interpret our reality.

One day, while contemplating this challenge to know the truth, I was reminded of an incident in 2004 in the outskirts of Toronto. I was convinced at the time that I knew the truth, so even though I struggled with thoughts of worry, fear, shame, guilt, and a plethora of other debilitating emotions, outwardly I appeared to have it all together.

Looking for direction and clarity over whether to accept an offer that would require uprooting my family and move to a different city, I decided to play a round of golf. I went to a course that I knew would not be busy, and booked a tee time when no one else was around. Standing with my driver in my hand on the first tee box, I noticed a gentleman by himself, sinking his putt to finish the first hole, almost 500 yards away from me. I deliberately took my time on that first hole—he could get a head start on the second hole, safely ahead of me, and there would be no pressure to play with him (which I did not want to do).

About ten minutes later, I arrived at the second hole tee box and noticed the same man sitting on the bench waiting for me. He asked if we could play together. Everything within me wanted to say no, but that would be rude, so I reluctantly agreed. And then I thought to myself, "If I'm not getting any time for quiet reflection on the golf course, at least I can preach to him and get him converted."

For the next four hours, I shared what I believed with him. But something strange happened while I was bombarding him with my "wealth" of knowledge regarding what I thought to be the truth. His manner of speaking was so different than mine. His beliefs didn't really match mine, but yet he possessed qualities that seemed to be missing in me. There was such a peace, patience, joy, kindness, compassion, generosity, and love about this man that I was completely taken aback.

How could he manifest these attributes if he didn't share my beliefs?

It wasn't that he stood against what I believed, but his relationship with the INFINITE was not based on a set of intellectual beliefs. There was just something that made him so alive—something that went beyond all thoughts and mental constructs. I left that round of golf confused and bewildered because with all my pedigree and ability to skillfully present what I believed, it felt like this man made a greater impact on me than I did on him.

Years later I reflected on this chance encounter. Religious beliefs are rooted in a dissatisfaction with the evil in the world. We intend to use our beliefs to provide a path out of humanity's state of dysfunction and defect. My goal that day on the golf course was to share my beliefs because I genuinely thought it would provide my fellow golfer freedom. The problem was that he demonstrated more freedom than I did. His freedom also revealed to me that my beliefs had become a way to strengthen my sense of self. In my mind, my beliefs made me right and the other golfer wrong.

After playing with this golfer for a while, it dawned on me that although I was intellectually an expert in my tradition's beliefs, my inner life didn't reflect the same peace, grace, and love that emanated from this man. Of course I didn't know what internal struggles he dealt with, but there was a calm and compassion in him that I had rarely seen before. I began to wonder whether I had made my belief system a mental idol that everyone had to follow.

> *Had I falsely assumed that a set of mental ideas and concepts about God was the truth?*
> *Had I taken the wisdom of spiritual texts and turned them into neatly packaged belief systems that in a way enhanced my sense of self more than set people free?*

After I experienced healing from cluster headaches in 2006, I still struggled with the emotional baggage rooted in the feeling that I'm not enough. But as I began to meditate on *divine love* on a more consistent basis, I noticed a significant shift in my consciousness. The mental and emotional pain disappeared, and I felt a perpetual peace and freedom unlike any I had experienced before. I began to awaken to a reality that I had never dared to consider…

Knowing the truth is not really a mental belief system, but an awareness of the *spirit* within.

Our *true self* is not the body, nor the thoughts of the mind, but the *spirit* that is one with God (or the Universe, if you prefer). To know the truth is to be aware of the *presence* within—not as a thought, but as the observer of thoughts. This presence is united with the larger infinite PRESENCE, and this union permeates with unconditional and selfless love. Out of this awareness, our sense of self can be transformed. The subconscious narrative of *I am not enough* is exchanged with an inner-awareness of *I am love!*

Some may ask, "Is this not a belief? What makes this inner-awareness different than any other religious belief system?" It's a good question, and I respond like this: a belief is a worldview, idea, or some other mental conception. So yes, it is true that so long as it only fills the pages of this book, this truth is a collection of thoughts that form a belief. Yet the experience of the awareness of *divine presence* is not a mental belief because it circumvents the mind. The distinction may seem immaterial at first, but when a person begins to awaken to their *true self*, the difference between mental-beliefs and inner-awareness is evident.

Although these mental ideas (often found in spiritual texts) are not themselves the truth, they can point us toward the truth. But the truth that sets us free is not a belief system, but a state of awareness of *presence*. It's a consciousness that is not grounded in your thinking mind, but in your *true self* that is one with God. Love is the fabric and substance of this union.

Jesus referred to this freedom as entering the kingdom of heaven. Paul called this salvation. Buddhism and Hinduism call it enlightenment. Other traditions call it transformation. No matter what you call it, something extraordinary happens when you move from fear to freedom. Just like the colorless tiger, when you remember that you are free, your real beauty is revealed, in all its colorful, sparkling glory. Peace, grace, and joy then infuse your being. You find the truth of who you are, and the purpose of your human experience.

2
WHAT IS LOVE?

Whenever you use the word *love*, you risk stepping on all kinds of landmines. Loaded with assumptions, expectations, and traditions, love is not easily defined because it means different things to different people at different times in their lives.

For many, love refers to the babe you married (until she wants to get divorced), the baby you gave birth to (until he grows up and slams the door in your face, telling you he hates you), the steakhouse down the road (until you become a vegan), or the dream job you worked hard to get (until you can't stand it because it runs your life). So what conclusion can we come to other than: love is complicated?

Love goes hand-in-hand with painful rejection. The man of your dreams tells you he loves you, and that he wants to spend the rest of his life with you, then goes out and cheats on you—with your best friend. When he gets caught, he returns to say, "I'm so sorry, baby. I love you, and it will never happen again."

Maybe the rejection comes from your dad. You know—the man who told you he loves you, and that you are the most important person in the world, but then forgot to show up to your dance recitals, and never got you a bike that one Christmas, even though he promised over and over again that he would.

With all the pain we associate with love, it seems as though love cannot really be trusted. But if you can't trust love, what *can* you trust?

This brings us to God. At some point in our lives, we've all seen a person holding a sign with some variation of the message *God loves you*, whether it's at a sporting event, parade, or street corner. The problem is that upon further scrutiny, many of these sign holders and the churches they represent depict God's love as quite selective and conditional, which makes it about as appealing as the "love" of certain narcissists we work to avoid. Compliance with doctrine, allegiance to the church, and a never-ending adoring worship are just some of the expectations that this God of "love" demands.

Judgment is another word frequently used in many religious circles. As you listen to some preachers, God will seem more angry than happy, more punishing than merciful, and more a personification of fear than of love. He reserves his biggest disdain for homosexuals, the Hollywood elite, and any other group that is dissimilar to a particular congregation. The target of his wrath is evident in the locations of the latest hurricanes, earthquakes, and other natural disasters. Judgment, by way of eternal punishment in a lake of fire, is the inevitable destination for all who refuse to believe the way they do.

Understandably, these stories we have been told about the *infinite* have only left us more bewildered about love. When left with our own thoughts, we can't help but wonder: if this judging and punishing God is synonymous with love, then love doesn't seem very appealing.

Therefore, to understand and trust love is a challenge for most of us. For millennia, the intrusive virus of fear has invaded the lens through which we see love and the ways in which our traditions interpret God and our relationship with the divine. From this viral fear, we have created the divisions and separations in the name of this God. Permeating our consciousness, fear has created an alternate reality wherein anxiety, craziness, and traumas seem more real than truth.

Amidst our chaos, there still remains a longing for *authentic* love. Love that is not toxic, not manipulative, not controlling, not fear-inducing, and not destructive, but instead makes us whole and complete.

Misconceptions About Love

To better understand love, let's first discuss a few misconceptions. Love is not a thought, or an action, or something we do. Certain beliefs can lead to *awareness* of love, but it's not love itself. Acting lovingly, such as helping a friend, is admirable, but it's not what love is. Often, but not always, doing good for others is the fruit of love—what love creates or how love performs. The action and the thoughts related to love, however, should not be confused with love itself.

Neither should love be considered an emotion, even though it exhibits many of the same patterns. Fundamentally, emotions are thoughts that create a sensation within you. In fact, the word *emotion* comes from the Latin equivalent **ēmōtus**, which means *to distract, disturb, agitate, stir up, move away, or move out*. Implied in the etymology is that your natural state is one of inner love, peace, and joy. Any experience or thought that drives you away from that state of peace is an emotion. Emotions essentially disturb the natural flow of love and shift your awareness from the present moment to dwelling on past experiences or future expectations.

So…What Is Love?

That still leaves us with the question: What is love? In short, love is energy. Of course defining love as energy doesn't sound very appealing. It just doesn't seem right to place love in the same category as your electricity bill and what you lack after running your first marathon. But consider how you felt when someone close to you got married or had a baby, or when you watched a musical performance that moved you to tears. You were caught up in the present moment, and felt a rush of exhilarating energy run through your body. The hairs on your arm stood up. You had goosebumps, and you felt incredibly alive. Amazingly, you felt one with the married couple, the baby, or the performer onstage. You experienced what they experienced, and felt pure joy and peace within. That's energy, and we call that energy *love*.

The findings of quantum physics show us that the universe is made up of energy, and that energy comes in many different forms, such as light, heat, gravitation, nuclear energy, and so on. Even the empty space that permeates the universe is not so empty after all, for it consists of dark energy and dark matter. No one knows for sure how dark energy and dark matter work, except that they somehow intelligently make the universe expand at a rapid rate and hold the universe together. Could it be that this invisible energy field that undergirds all existence is love—a love that is the source of all life? If so, what is this fundamental force or energy that could be described as love?

The Heart of the Conscious Presence…

Consider that quantum physics also demonstrates that all particles and objects are intricately linked to the presence of an observer or consciousness. In other words, matter is not so much carbon that has been scrambled together by pure chance with a few other elements, but it is instead the manifestation of life through a conscious presence. What I'm suggesting is that the heart of this conscious presence is love. That love is the fundamental energy that generates new life and moves all life in the universe toward consciousness of unity and oneness.

This leads us to ancient texts. Long before we put giant satellites in space, before we invented the internet, the iPhone, and the television, great thinkers tried to make sense of humanity's existence. Relying more deeply on their intuition than on scientific data, they studied nature and observed the wind, rain, sky, sun, and everything in between. All of it communicated the ways of the infinite. These philosophers often spoke of their gods as spirits, which in many traditions also means *wind* or *breath*. In other words, they recognized that the energy permeating the empty space was not so empty after all, but it bore witness to an invisible divine *presence*.

By the time Jesus came on the scene, this view of the spirit was not only commonly accepted, but it was downright foundational for many religions. Some Greek philosophers, such as Epimenides, spoke of all people having our being in God. David, the psalmist, made the same assertion by suggesting that he could not run away from God, because even when he made his bed in hell, God was still there.

Jesus then added a new dimension to this perception of the divine. God was indeed the *spirit* (consciousness) that permeated the universe. But this unseen God was not an impersonal consciousness to be afraid of, but instead was the *father* of us all. By presenting God as *father*, Jesus made God more relatable to the human mind. Jesus then demonstrates that this relationship with the *father* was one of love. Later, as his followers reflected upon what they observed in Jesus, they concluded that God is *spirit* (consciousness) and *love* (energy). Their conclusion seems to match what quantum physics hints at and what many of us intuitively feel: Love is the fundamental energy of the universe - the essence of the spiritual presence in all things.

Pierre Teilhard de Chardin, a French philosopher and Jesuit priest who passed away in 1955, tied this spiritual presence or mystery to the beginning of the universe. He proposed that love is the energy at the heart of the Big Bang, deeply embedded in the universe as the *cosmological force*.[1] In other words, love is the integrated energy field, the substance of the infinite observer that is the source of life.

Without love as the ether of the universe, our place in it is void of meaning. But with love as the principal energy force of life, the purpose of our existence is to awaken to that dimension within us that is love.

Love's Connection To Oneness and Unity

Whenever we talk about the true meaning of love, its link with *unity* or *oneness* is unavoidable. For instance, we might think of love as being synonymous with the union between our parents that results in our conception. Then the nine months of our prenatal existence is spent in oneness with our mother's womb. In the early stages of our post-birth life, our mothers nursed us, creating a bond—or union—that often lingers for the remainder of our life. We consider this relationship between mother and child an example of love because of the union they share.

A similar bond is also apparent when your dog or cat snuggles up to you. You feel the energy of your union with your furry friends and call it love. Sitting in a restaurant with your friends can be filled with a comparable energy. You feel a sense of belonging, or oneness, with your friends, and again we call it love.

My son, Nathanael, once told me that attending a Coldplay concert at the Rose Bowl was a spiritual experience. The energy was palatable, and he felt a oneness with the thousands of people that sat enraptured by a live rendition of "A Head Full of Dreams." The experience brought him to both tears and laughter. The reason is simple: sharing a moment of unity with so many people opened his heart to become conscious of love.

According to our spiritual traditions, marriage is the union of a couple, where two people become one. The success of a marriage is, of course, not guaranteed with the simple signing of a license. Instead, the marital success is a result of the strength of the union the couple shares. When the sense of oneness is strengthened, energy flows from that union and creates positive change around the couple.

When we first met our life partner, we fell in love through a series of moments of accepting each other for who we are. We shared ourselves—emotionally, mentally, physically and spiritually—by exposing our flaws, our insecurities, and our weaknesses. Our mutual acceptance silenced the nagging inner voice that told us that we may not be enough. In that way, we became conscious of love.

On the deepest level, love is oneness with the divine, which creates a union that dispels our fixation with ourselves. What seems to be "out there" is really one with what's "in here."

The Equivalency of Love and One in Hebrew Texts

This leads us to a fascinating ancient Jewish concept. Stay with me here, because this brief and puzzling bit of information is mostly for the ancient literature nerds.

The Hebrew word for *one* is *ehad*, and the word for *love* is *ahavah*. In mystical numerology (*gematriyya*), each Hebrew letter has a numerical value.

The *gematriyya* of *ehad* is the sum of its individual letters:

1 (*alef*) + 8 (*het*) + 4 (*dalet*) = 13.

The *gematriyya* of *ahavah* is 1 (*alef*) + 5 (*heh*) + 2 (*bet*) + 5 (*heh*) = 13.

As you can see, oneness and love are equivalent.

Together *ehad* and *ahavah* add up to 26.

This is the same numerical value assigned to the Jewish holiest divine name: *YHVH*, the sum of whose letters (10+5+6+5) also equals 26. God is oneness and love.[2]

In the Christian tradition, Jesus gives us some practical examples of what that connection between oneness and love looks like. For example, Jesus told us to love our neighbors *as* ourself. Notice the precision of his language: he didn't tell us to love them as much as we love ourselves, but to actually love them *as if they were us*.

Another time, Jesus told his followers that what you do to the "least of these" you do unto me. The Father was in Jesus, and Jesus was in the prisoners, the strangers, the naked, the hungry, the thirsty, and the sick.

The point is that love and oneness are inextricably connected. Love is the invisible energy-field of the universe. It's the divine *presence* within us that moves us toward awareness of our shared union.

Every movement toward unity, whether it's with our children, pets, friends, partners, neighbors, or even our enemies, is a moment of awakening to the divine essence of love that rests within us. It's the divine manifesting through form, revealing our oneness.

The Challenge Of Perceiving Oneness

But I get it. This universal *oneness* is a challenge for our dual minds to comprehend. Since childhood, we have been taught that there's a dividing line between *me* and *what's out there*. If, for example, we were to ask "Where is the universe?" instinctively we would perceive the universe as outside of us. This seems reasonable to the mind, but is it accurate? Of course not. Our essence does not exist as a separate entity from the universe, for we are a part of the whole. We are *one* with the universe, because the universe is *one*.

Our *oneness* is not just a logical assumption and a spiritual concept. Physicist Fritjof Capra says that quantum physics "reveals a basic oneness of the universe. It shows that we cannot decompose the world into independently existing smaller units. As we penetrate into matter, nature does not show us any isolated basic building blocks (like we once thought) but rather appears as a complicated web of relations between the various parts of the whole."[3]

The challenge for us is that we don't recognize that *oneness* because our ego-mind is limited in its perception, and makes a distinction between self and non-self.

Herein lies a clue to how we become conscious of love. What I mean is that we are aware of love when we move beyond the limitations of the ego-mind and awaken within to our oneness with what's outside our form. We identify with "otherness" as being us through forgiveness, compassion, non-judgment, kindness, and empathy, and thus become aware of the transcending presence of love.

How Fear Opposes Love…

One way to better understand love is by contrasting it with fear. While love is the equivalent of one or unity, fear is the equivalent of two, or separation. Fear originates in the mind as thoughts that are not cognizant of the union we share. It's a toxic energy, or perhaps even more succinctly, an emotional pain you experience when you are unaware of unconditional love. The separation that the mind perceives through the five senses gives rise to the concept of *me* and *them*. The consequence of this apparent separation is fear.

As unlikely as it sounds, I'm reminded of a shopping center near my home in San Diego. *(Stay with me here through the strangeness of this story. There's a point here. I promise.)*

Walking through the mall, I observed everything around me, including the beauty and charm of the people all around me. At the food court, I exchanged pleasantries with a cashier as I paid for my lunch. As we spoke, I thought of my connection with her as a human being. I considered that in ways beyond the perceptions of my five senses she was one with me. The divine *presence* was in her even if she was not aware of it. Being present in the moment with her and providing her my undivided attention and her reciprocating created a moment of laughter.

As I walked away, my attention was drawn to all the people milling around the mall. For a moment it seemed like I observed everyone in a "caught up" spiritual state. Everyone was heading somewhere, apparently ignorant of our oneness beyond visible matter. I know it sounds like I'm drunk on hippie juice, but I became cognizant of my union with these strangers, and how all of us were one in a nonphysical dimension. I was overwhelmed with gratitude and peace and knew that no matter where my thoughts would take me, love was the essence of the *spirit* and consciousness permeating the universe.

A few moments later, I saw an elderly Hispanic woman. I tried to catch her gaze, but her eyes were glossed over. Similar to a young child wandering in search of her mother, this woman seemed lost in her head. I'm not sure what she was thinking, but I knew her mind was somewhere other than focused on what was in front of her. I looked around at the other faces in the crowd. Everywhere I looked, I noticed similar almost-hypnotized expressions. They were not aware of the union and source of life that permeates all existence.

Leaving the mall that day, I considered the tragic error of fear. The mind infected by fear perceives only separation. It's unable to recognize our shared oneness with one another. We view each other with reservation, even as a threat, a competition, an enemy that we must guard against, and keep at a distance. This perception of separation results in suffering —an inner hell filled with anxiety, worry, jealousy, depression, and feelings of rejection.

Another downfall of thoughts rooted in fear is separation from what is present. Fear essentially refuses to live in union with what is. Love experiences life because it's one with life. Fear avoids life because it cannot be at peace with it.

In this preoccupied fearful state, our thoughts are consumed with our successes and failures. We relive the triumphs of yesterday because what is present does not satisfy us. We recall our failures because they provide a pretext for the apparent lack in the present.

These memories then become the compass of our future. Projecting our past onto our future, we are unable to come to terms with experiencing life in the now.

The success of the past turns to greed, compulsiveness, possessiveness, and an unhealthy need for power, pushing us further away from awareness of our oneness. Our sense of identity is no longer attached to love's all-embrace, but instead to our accomplishments and our victories. We think that losing what we achieved in the past would diminish our value. The threat we feel inside that we are not enough anymore, therefore, turns into a compulsive pursuit of fame, money, power, and sex. When our misguided identity and false self comes under attack, we lash out in anger, hypocrisy, and intolerance of what we perceive as other from us.

The failures of the past, on the other hand, turn to guilt, anger, regrets, and feelings of rejection. As we identify with our disappointments and letdowns, we become victims in our minds. To avoid or alleviate some of the emotional pain of not feeling good enough, we complain about how unfairly we have been treated, and how misunderstood we are. In this world of *us versus them*, we assign blame and fault to our enemies—anything to silence the nagging doubts inside that we are not enough. The doubts, of course, can never be stopped entirely—no matter how many new toys we buy in the mall—so we unconsciously punish ourselves with anxiety, worry, depression, and even sickness.

Fear has gained control of our minds. Oneness with the Source has been forgotten. We are trapped alone with our thoughts, left wondering how we can be free from the torment of loneliness and the despair we feel.

Love Revealed In A Story

Jesus was masterful at telling stories that conveyed a deeper meaning. They were called parables because they communicated in the language of metaphors that people related to. One such parable is about the relationship between a father and his two sons.

The younger son—perhaps disappointed with his lot in life, and maybe in search of greater significance—one day asked his father for his share of the inheritance. Asking for the money, the grand piano, and the Maserati (yes, I'm taking my creative liberties here and adding my own twist to an ancient story) in advance of his father's passing was the epitome of selfishness and in opposition to all decency and sensibility. Jesus' audience would have been seething with anger toward this young man.

> *What a spoiled brat! What a loser! What a _____ (you decide this one)!*

The young son was entitled, selfish, and deserved to get nothing—no stocks, no real estate, and definitely no cryptocurrency. The older son, on the other hand, was a workaholic and always earned his keep. I'm sure everyone in the audience (blinded by hypocrisy) would have first identified with the hard-working older brother. So when Jesus told his audience that the father gave the younger son the entire share of the inheritance, it must have caused shock and outrage.

> *Who responds like that to a self-centered and self-absorbed son?*

> No one...except this father!

Jesus was, of course, speaking about something much deeper than a male with two feet, two legs, two hands, a wrinkled face, and a long grey beard. He was speaking about the SOURCE OF LIFE. The word *father* was understood to imply the originator and the transcending *being* of the universe; the one that they also called Yahweh.

The god they had heard about was not like this father. Their god was more like them: ready to cut off all rebellion at its source with zero tolerance for blatant disobedience. So when Jesus presents the father as generous and kind even to this ungrateful son, he confronted every fear within them that suggested that such action would make them appear weak, too lenient to a rebellious child. Jesus also challenged every preconceived notion they had about God as quick to judge, and instead presented the divine father as infinitely (and scandalously) loving, tolerant, compassionate, and accepting.

Jesus' story then took flight on a familiar trajectory. After the father gave his inheritance to the younger son, financial recession unlike any other set in and the son's investments collapsed. The young son, drunk on his remaining millions, then squandered the rest of his inheritance on wild living.

The great recession had also taken its toll on the job market. Good paying jobs had vanished, so in the hope of eating the scraps left behind at the local farm, the younger son took a job feeding pigs.

Drowning in guilt, insecurity, and all kinds of fear, he had nothing left to live for. It was an excellent place for him to come to his senses. He remembered his father's generosity, and decided to return home to ask for a job.

The crowd must have sat in rapt suspense as they listened to Jesus. How would the father respond to the return of his ungrateful and backstabbing son?

What do you say to a spoiled brat who wants nothing to do with you, demands his inheritance while you are still alive, and then, when he loses everything, conveniently wants to come back home? You'd probably call your lawyer and make sure that he has no legal claim on anything else in your home, and then you throw him out.

But the son knew he had messed up. What could he tell his father to gain some kind of favor? He needed a stellar opening line, something that would both signal his change of heart and convince his dad to give him a job. He decided to tell his father that he was a true failure and he was unworthy of being a son, and promised to work hard if his father let him back on his payroll. So the son memorized his lines and set off on his journey back home.

As the son edged his way onto his father's land, the father saw him and his heart filled with compassion. Out of instinctual love, the father ran toward his son and embraced him, kissing him before the son had a chance to say a word. Overwhelmed by the love, the son blurted out his memorized lines about being sorry, but the words seemed irrelevant to the father, who got his son the best Armani suit, put the family heirloom ring on his finger, and put a pair of Jason of Beverly Hills shoes on his feet (or something like that). Then he called all of the A-listers from the adjacent lands (and every other list, from B to Z, because what else would love do?) together for a big celebration.

The story that Jesus told is full of shocking assertions about scandalous love. Mythological in nature, the story upended every notion people had about God. Their minds had created a god predicated on their fears and shame. But the originator—THE SOURCE OF LIFE—was something much grander: the father's essence is love, and that love is oneness between the source and its creation.

When the son wandered off in rebellion, he didn't cease being a son. He just wasn't aware of it anymore. He falsely assumed that because of his guilt he was unworthy of a union with his father.

Even the older son, despite his faithful service, was unaware of his union with his father. Intellectually he knew he was a son, but on a deeper level, the older son acted like a servant, and therefore didn't truly know who he was. Fear had distorted his perception, and consequently, he was unable to see the oneness with his father and his brother.

The fear in our minds has made us wander away from our shared oneness. Much like Jesus' audience when he told this story, our preconceived ideas about God are based on an illusion of fear.

If we want better lives and to enjoy a healthier new Earth, our fears must be driven out by awakening to love. Our individual and collective happiness, health, and success depend on it. More importantly: the planet Earth and the beauty of its creation depend upon our return to love—a love that is void of fear and rooted in the oneness of all.

3

STAGES OF CONSCIOUSNESS

In the evening, we go to bed, close our eyes, blanket both our bodies and minds, and wait for our waking consciousness to fade. While we sleep, we are unaware of time, our body, and our surroundings. We spend about one-third of our lives in this state of limited mobility with minimal responses to our environment. Nothing in our biology changes at night, but we are not aware of our reality because we are asleep.

Similarly, most of humanity is asleep—unconscious of our *true self*. Unaware of who we really are, the source of our existence, the purpose of life, and the divine love that is embedded in all of us.

Our current state of unawareness reminds me of the story of a farmer...

While walking through the forest one day, the farmer found a young eagle that had fallen out of its nest. Feeling sorry for the injured bird, he brought it home and left it in the farmyard with his chickens. It did not take long for the king of birds to regain strength and grow. But confined to the pen, it had adopted the behaviors and eating habits of the chickens.

An environmentalist passed by the farm one day and, noticing the majestic bird in the yard, asked the farmer what an eagle was doing among the chickens. The farmer replied that the eagle had never learned how to fly. It had been surrounded by chickens most of its life, so it ate like a chicken, clucked like a chicken, and walked like a chicken.

"I'd say that bird is more chicken than eagle now," the farmer said.

"But its true identity is still as an eagle," the environmentalist said. "It just needs to wake up to what it really is!"

Similarly, we, as humanity, need to wake up to who we are. The chaos created by our unconsciousness is evident everywhere. Greed, hatred, bigotry, homophobia, xenophobia, misogyny, racial intolerance, violence, and wars are just some of the negative symptoms of humanity's unconscious state. Like the eagle that thinks it is a chicken, we need to awaken the gift of conscious flight that lay dormant within us.

But how can we awaken, what does it mean to be conscious, and are there different types of consciousness? Let's explore this concept of consciousness a bit further.

What Is Consciousness?

Losing a loved one is perhaps the most painful experience we go through as humans. It's often surreal to look at the body of a family member or friend and realize that they have passed away. Usually, we refer to their death in euphemisms: "Their spirit has parted from their body," or "Their consciousness has left their body." As our language would suggest, we seem to know intuitively that what made them a living being was not their body itself, but an inexplicable presence within that physical form.

Needless to say, human consciousness has bewildered philosophers, scientists, theologians, and spiritual thinkers for millennia. When science dissects your essence, it does an excellent job of explaining the blood, the guts, and the other gory insides. It also magnificently explains the fascinating world of atoms, molecules, and cells that form the patterns that make up *you*. Yet science is not adept at giving answers to why you fall in love, why you want your life to matter, and why you are conscious of your own existence. Consciousness, therefore, stands as an unsolved mystery even for the greatest scientific minds.

In search for answers to the question of human consciousness, seventeenth century French philosopher Rene' Descartes coined the term, "I think; therefore I am." The ability to think was evidence of our consciousness to Descartes. But this placed an excessive emphasis on thoughts. Even a computer can store data, and make logical conclusions based on that data. In other words, even a computer can think. Yet it doesn't have the ability to *experience* reality or life. It does not possess the same sense of presence and personal awareness that we enjoy as humans.

Recent scientific studies indicate that many animals also have consciousness even though it's different from humans. For instance, our little dog, Pumpkin (who, I must note, my family named without my consent) has a different awareness than me. She cannot recognize herself in a mirror, but she is conscious of herself by smelling her own feces (I'm happy that's not a human quality). Even the little lizard that runs around my garden in the summertime possesses a form of consciousness. How do I know?

Because when I move toward it, it runs away from me. So the dog and the lizard are both conscious, but their type of consciousness differs from ours.

Then, as we have discussed, within the standard twenty-four-hour cycle of a day we experience uniquely opposing types of consciousness: awake and asleep. But the various types of perception do not end there, because some people are subject to an abnormal state of consciousness (such as a personality disorder) and others still may enter an altered awareness where addictions control their thoughts.

So what is consciousness? No words seem adequate enough to completely describe the depth of the mystery of consciousness. Yet, words such as a *presence*, a personal *awareness* and an inward *witness* come to mind. Perhaps the best definition is found in what consciousness grants us. What I mean is that being conscious gives us the ability to OBSERVE REALITY and EXPERIENCE LIFE.

And that's an important distinction, because, as we are exploring throughout this book, our consciousness is either grounded in love, or darkened by fear. We observe reality and experience life either through the egoic mind (with its underlying fear that *I am not enough the way I am*), or through the spirit that is aware (through the manifestation of love) of its union with *everything*. In other words, whatever stage of consciousness we are in shapes our reality and determines what we experience.

Stages of Human Consciousness

As humans, it's possible to move from one level of consciousness to another. We mature in love and union, and enter a new phase of awareness. Each stage is a step toward more complete wholeness and inclusiveness. Once we have crossed into a new consciousness, it's nearly impossible to return to a less inclusive awareness. Although the following stages of consciousness will often overlap (and are therefore not necessarily linear in development) they form a basis by which we can understand the current levels of human consciousness.

The most primal human consciousness is what we refer to as EGOCENTRIC, where people are oblivious to other people's feelings and thoughts. They act in their own best interest and have very little awareness of how others perceive things. A person at the egocentric stage often thinks, "Whatever is right for me is what matters," or, "I don't care about her—I'm doing what's best for me." The most extreme displays of egocentric consciousness are found among outright narcissists, who lack any empathy or compassion for others. Many are even capable of heinous crimes and violent behavior as a result of this egocentrism.

The next stage of consciousness is ETHNOCENTRIC. At this level, the person has evolved from complete self-centeredness to tribal sentience, where they are mindful of what's in the best interest of the group they belong to, such as family, church, business, race, religion, political party, and nation. They may even be willing to lay down their life for their clan. However, people displaying this type of awareness generally compartmentalize the world into "us versus them," "in or out," or "friend or enemy." This can create tension, conflict, and at times even violence and war. Although it's a step up from the egocentric consciousness, this level has the potential for even more evil because it easily turns into a form of collective egocentricity. And since the potential destruction is done in the name of a "righteous" cause—whether political, religious, racial, or national—people within the group feel justified in doing harm to other groups because it serves the group's greater good.

The third stage in human consciousness is WORLD-CENTRIC. Here people are more concerned with equality among all groups of people. Freedom of expression and freedom of choice are considered the rights of every person. Issues such as protecting the Earth, eliminating social and economic disparity, and reversing the ongoing mass extinctions are fundamental within a world-centric awareness. Where a world-centric perception often fails is in empathy and compassion toward those whose views are dissimilar to their own. So even though it is more inclusive than ethnocentric consciousness, individuals who propagate a world-centric consciousness fall into many of the same egoic traits exemplified in the egocentric and ethnocentric perceptions.

Higher Stage of Consciousness

The highest stage of known human consciousness is CHRIST-CENTRIC. I don't use the word Christ here to identify with a religious group or to ascribe higher virtue to Christianity than other religions. If my background was different, I'm sure the name would likely reflect that in my word choice. The point for now is that the word is less important than what it represents.

Since I will devote an entire section in a later chapter to the Hebrew roots of Christ and how they became connected with Jesus, for now I will just give a brief definition. Christ is the incarnation of the divine *logos* in visible matter — the union of matter with spirit. In a sense, the entire universe is the embodiment of Christ. Yet Christ is also the incarnation of God in humanity — the union of the human with the divine.

Therefore, a Christ-centric consciousness is when you are aware in your heart, soul, and mind of this union. You are conscious of Christ in you. You observe and experience Christ in everything. And you identify with everything as Christ.

Love is the heart of this awareness. The mystics speak of it as the consciousness of oneness with the *absolute*, the *infinite*, or what we commonly refer to as God. When one is aware of this union, the lines between what is "in here" and what's "out there" are blurred. So-called otherness diminishes to the point of dissolution. One becomes aware of selfless love as the energy that holds all things together. While egocentric, ethnocentric, and world-centric consciousness are all rooted in egoic awareness, the Christ-centric consciousness is anchored in the eternal reality beyond our minds and physical forms.

The human mind is naturally cynical that such a consciousness is possible. It cannot comprehend it any more than our cat understands why we dance to Beyoncé and tear up while watching the *Titanic*. We are fundamentally incapable of grasping this kind of awareness unless we awaken to it. In the words of Jesus, we are not capable of seeing the "kingdom of God" within us unless we become born again (awakened).

Many people, whether religious or not, never awaken to their Christ-centric consciousness. They may experience momentary glimpses of who they are and what that state of being may offer. They may even have ideas of a better life based on love, happiness, and peace. But it's easier to reject or criticize something than to acknowledge and confront your issues. So cynicism, disillusionment, intellectual pride, arrogance, and bitterness stain their perception.

Yet there are others who open their eyes and catch a glimpse of something bigger than themselves. Perhaps we feel a *presence*, experience something unexplainable, or are moved by selfless love.

There are also times when a nightmare awakens us to this higher consciousness. Maybe it's the loss of a job, a breakup, a divorce, an illness, or the death of a loved one. The sting of the night's terrible vision haunts us and compels us to find grace to silence our pain and love to heal our wounds. That is the beginning of an awakening to our *true self*.

Your True Self…

Since your *true self* is a Christ-centric consciousness not rooted in thoughts, the concept of *true self* is a challenge to define by rational thought. How can you explain something that we cannot perceive with the five senses? The words we use inevitably fall short, and what the mind cannot easily explain it categorizes as mystery. We are frightened by a reality that our minds cannot wrap around.

Perhaps this is why most of humanity runs away from what lies deep within us. Look at Christianity, my own tradition. When some of the followers of Jesus came to the empty tomb, they were afraid and bewildered. A resurrected Jesus was a challenge to their preconceived notions of reality. It was much easier to deal with death than a new kind of life. Their response to the mystery before them was to flee.

For centuries, western Christianity has been running away from the *presence* of God in each of us, choosing instead to follow a narrative of inherent evil in humanity. Of course, hidden in the Christian spiritual texts is an opposing story, that says we are inherently blessed -- connected with the SOURCE OF LIFE. When fear injected itself in the human race, our minds became unaware of the divine within us, prioritizing whatever the five senses communicated to us, rather than the inner essence of our being.

But as the book of Genesis poetically and perhaps metaphorically describes, humanity became a living being when God (later defined as love) breathed life into our nostrils. Without this invisible breath, spirit, energy, and consciousness, only dust would remain.

Of course, this seems bizarre to our rational and deductive minds. But isn't this whole thing we call the universe a bit strange? In fact, you don't have to go much further than yourself to be in awe of the wonder of the human experience. Remember: you were once a child (unless you are like me, and your family still thinks you are one), and now you're an adult who's developing, evolving, and expanding in more ways than one. You are a marvelous mystery that even the brightest minds are unable to understand. (No wonder your significant other hasn't figured you out yet.)

Yet, suggesting that God lies within you while still transcending all things poses a challenge to our logical minds. *How can everyone be one with a God, whose essence is love, when there is so much evil and dysfunction in humanity?* It's a perfectly valid question, one that we will continue to explore in this book.

What we do know is that many traditions speak of this union of the divine and the human.

What did they know? What had they experienced that might lend some insight into our important question?

The writings and teachings of Paul, the most prolific writer and teacher within Christianity, consistently point to this union. While speaking to a group of philosophers and nature worshippers in Athens, he quotes some of their poets: "In God, we live, move and have our being."[1] Writing to people who lived in a region called Ephesus, he explores this idea further when he says "the Father is over all, through all and in all."[2] In another place, he writes that "Christ is all and in all,"[3] although we are unable to see it until our hearts have awakened to our *true self*.

Paul then speaks of a mystery that the human mind had failed to comprehend for ages until Jesus revealed it. That mystery was "Christ in you."[4] This union had always been present, but it was hidden from our minds. Only a few paragraphs later, he explains that Christ is the embodiment of the divine in human form.

Of course, this doesn't explain the evil in the world, or our propensity for selfishness. But Paul makes clear that evil exists because the mind has alienated itself from God. Evil, therefore is simply a byproduct of becoming unconscious of the unifying Life—BEING, LOVE, SPIRIT—that fills the universe. (This leads to all kinds of questions that we will delve into later.)

If, for now, we accept Paul's writings, then we must conclude that the mind is not conscious of the oneness of all life. Unaware of the love as the unifying energy of the universe, it is lost in fear's illusion. We are asleep and unconscious of our *true self*, and thus under the grip of disillusioned dreams, nightmares, and false perceptions.

So as we explored earlier, the mind is therefore not where awakening begins. Instead, we must wake up to the divine reality beyond our intellect, and in our spirit—the true essence of our being.

The good news is that when you are aware of this transcending, beautiful, and authentic oneness with the GROUND OF BEING, your mind is also transformed. Your mind becomes aligned with your *true self*. New thoughts, feelings, and attitudes that create life, beauty, and happiness will then naturally emerge.

The Rest of the Story...

We began this chapter with a story about the eagle that was unconscious of its true identity. So let us end with the rest of the story...

When the environmentalist found the eagle among the chickens, he took the majestic bird in his hands, raised it toward the sky and said, "You belong to the sky. Spread your wings and fly."

Instead of flying toward the horizon in freedom, the eagle saw the chickens eating their food, and swooped back down to join them. Not giving up quickly, the environmentalist brought the bird up with him on the farmhouse rooftop, held it high and said, "You are not a chicken. You're an eagle. Spread your wings and fly." But the eagle, fearful and unaware of its identity and potential, jumped down once again and joined the chickens.

Finally, the environmentalist brought the eagle to a mountain. Holding the bird up above his head, he urged once more, "You're an eagle! Spread your wings and fly." The eagle looked around in search of the farmyard, but instead caught a glimpse of the sun peeking through the clouds. With eyes firmly fixed on the sun appearing through the parting clouds, the eagle slowly began to spread its wings. Then, with an exultant screech, it soared effortlessly into the sky. Far above the farmyard, the eagle found its true identity, infinite life, and purpose.

Perhaps you have also been conditioned to live as something you are not. Maybe you have been assigned artificial labels of who you are by your family, friends, religion, and culture. The dimension in you that is one with God has been hidden by the clouds of fear, shame, rejection, and guilt. But there is a light within you. As you catch a glimpse of the brightness of divine love, you will find your *true self* and soar to new heights.

So my friend, *wake up to who you are*. You're not the sum of your biology, the collection of your thoughts, or a chicken in a farmyard. You are a soaring, majestic spirit -- one with the essence of the same energy that permeates the universe: *love*.

PART II

THE FALSE SELF

Your egoic false self is who you *think* you are, but your thinking does not make it true.

— RICHARD ROHR

4

THE FORMATION OF THE EGO

Now that we've explored the foundational pathway to finding our *true self*, we'll talk in more depth about the cause of our emotional and mental pain. We will look with new eyes on old wisdom and gain insight into how fear, guilt, insecurity, anxiety, shame, depression, addictions, and obsessive thinking entrench themselves in our minds. We will also study everyday examples that reinforce false narratives about who we are.

Let's begin with the word *I*. In the same way that there is real and fake news, there's also the real and the fake *I*. Understanding this false *I* provides a clue to what is really holding us back from happiness, peace, and love.

The word *I* (along with its close relatives, *me, my,* and *mine*) is not only a simple pronoun that we learn as children, but it is also central to what keeps us trapped in our heads. Learning and mastering *I* begins early in life. Born with an innate sense of union with our mother, and maybe even an awareness of the divine within us, it doesn't take long before we forget the oneness that we share. Shifting from a deep spiritual awareness of love to a consciousness based primarily on what we perceive with our five senses, we suffer a form of amnesia. The innocence with which we ran around naked while our mom or dad chased after us is replaced with a demand for our own privacy. Why? Because of the fear that we have learned. We gain self-awareness and perceive ourselves as separate and different from our parents, siblings, and friends.

Our conception of *I* is so intrusive to our consciousness that when our brother reaches out for the toy we received for Christmas, we quickly fight back and lay claim to it with a distinct admonishment: "(That's) *mine.*" In fact, the first time we master a complete sentence it's likely to begin with *I* or contain the words *me* or *my*.

The word *I* comes from the Latin word *ego*, and it was also used in ancient Greek texts. For example, the Greek New Testament uses *I* (the ego) as the antitype of Christ. When we think of the word *ego*, we often associate it with someone who is full of himself, but the true definition is broader. The word can best be interpreted as self-identity, sense of self, and the conceptualized self. Implied in our understanding of the word *ego* is that *I* is separated from *others*, which in turn results in identification with your thoughts and body. Another interesting definition is that the ego is a consciousness that has "Edged God Out," suggesting that identification with our thoughts has made us unaware of our spirit, which is one with the *infinite*.

So the concept of *I*, or the ego, is essentially the mind's characterization of what distinguishes me from what is perceived as "out there." It's the mind's answer to the "Who am I?" question based on labels, masks, and judgments. It's how we experience reality when we are unaware of our union with God.

Conditioned Since Childhood

Our identification with the ego began when we were children. We were born into a family with a last name, we were given a first name, then placed in a race and gender category, and distinguished by height, hair and eye color, and a plethora of other distinguishable physical features. We were later grouped according to age, appearance, athleticism, creativity, intelligence, ethnicity, religion, and even the socioeconomic status of our parents. The sum of all these concepts turned into a mental construct of who we are. We began to identify with our thoughts, which we linked together to form the subconscious beliefs that shaped how we view the world and what we do with the life we have.

Embryonic to this conscious mental construct of ourselves is an underlying unconscious fearful feeling that we are not enough the way we are. When *I*—the independent and separated self—became a concept in our young minds, it also ignited a craving for love. The oneness of love that initially pervaded our consciousness faded as we gained a mental idea of self. Love is no longer associated with the union that we participate in and that makes up our *true self*. Instead, love has become an egoic pursuit that *I* have to earn or deserve.

Subconsciously, the egoic mind, therefore, begins to look for ways to be loved. Since we spend so much time with our parents and our siblings in those early years, we take on traits similar to theirs in an attempt to gain their love and acceptance. To hide our insecurity and shame, we create a false self that the ego assumes will be accepted and approved. We shape ourselves into whomever we think we must be to earn love.

Maybe that's why we spend so much time carefully curating our Instagram and Facebook profiles. Taking a hundred selfies and winnowing them down to one, we apply the right filter, and then upload the photo in hopes of reaching a record-breaking number of likes.

Needless to say, the more we try to create a persona that we think will be accepted and loved, the more we actually reinforce the mental narrative of separation from love. Love is no longer the oneness that we share with God and one another, but instead becomes the pursuit of the ego.

The conceptualized self has exchanged awareness of the union of love with earning love and acceptance based on how well we can perform. As children, we therefore obsessively ask our parents for their approval:

Did I do good, Dad?

Do I look good, Mom?

Are you proud of me?

Experiencing reality through a fearful perception, we want answers to the ego's nagging unconscious prodding: "Am I enough for love?"

How Egoic Patterns Remain, Even As We Age

The voice within us is unrelenting, and drives us to perform for love (even after the death of our parents). The egoic mind has convinced us that we must become worthy of love rather than merely become aware of the union of love we already share. So our entire life is then consumed with an unconscious pursuit of love and acceptance from our parents, and often the god our parents worshipped. This deep inner craving for love influences our personality in very complicated ways.

Since being successful is a way to validate our conceptualized self as deserving of love, we may pursue success in areas that we unconsciously perceive will please our parents. Whether through sports, academics, arts, technology, social connectivity, or some form of creative expression, we look to strengthen our ego's identity by seeking experiences, careers, and lifestyles that give us the most attention, respect, and recognition.

And if we were raised in a home where our parents were unfulfilled in their own lives, they may have sought their fulfillment through our accomplishments. This may have created insecurity in us as children, influencing our interests early on and throughout our lives.

Many of us may have also been continually criticized at home, unfavorably compared to a sibling, or bullied at school, which created a stressful childhood. As adults, these experiences now contribute to making lifestyle and career choices that lead to further stress. The reason why is quite evident: we have convinced ourselves that finding acceptance and love are linked with stressful circumstances.

A child growing up in a home with alcoholism or abuse may develop an overly care-taking ego, having learned that the parent's needs came first and their erratic behavior required compliance. While in an emotionally neglectful household, illness may be a way for a child to gain needed attention. In this case, the egoic pattern throughout their life is based on being physically and emotionally weak as a way to get others to show them compassion and care.

Even if we are raised in loving families, we cannot completely escape the ego's hold on our subconscious. Because as children we will at some point invariably experience rejection or distress.

Coded into our subconscious, these negative feelings then guide us throughout our lives.

When we fail to live up to the standards that the ego has created for being worthy of love, we may turn to drugs or alcohol to numb the pain we feel or get involved with some self-absorbed or even illicit activity to get back at the haters—that may include joining a gang, cult, or sect that makes us feel accepted. At some point, unless we first end up in prison or even dead from our addictions, we may come to our senses and realize the deception we are in. We may then look for love from a partner who we think will complete us, perhaps start living vicariously through our children, or maybe even turn to religion for certainty.

The ego's search for acceptance and love is constant. Never able to escape the perpetual fear that it may not be enough for love, the ego is the cause of the inner suffering we experience.

The Day I Was Humiliated

When I was a teenager attending school in Sweden, I had a teacher who performed a reading experiment with my class. She claimed that one can test a person's ability to read by how many times they move their eyes while reading a line in a book.

"A great reader," she said, "can read an entire line in a book while only moving their eyes once. An average reader can read a line with no more than two movements of their eyes. Anything more than two eye movements is below average."

I made two eye movements of my own in that moment: one nervous look to the student on my right, and another anxious glance to the student on my left.

She continued on. "Now, open to page 225 in your books. I will go around the room and test each of you individually to observe how many times you shift your eyes to read one line."

Luckily for me, she started at the opposite end of the classroom, making me one of the last students to be examined. I was both excited and nervous. I thought I was smarter than the other students, yet I also struggled with the insecurity that I was not enough. Holding these two egoic opposites in my mind, I nervously waited for my turn.

By the time the teacher arrived at my desk, all the students had either moved their eyes once or twice. Even the student we ignorantly considered a slow-witted outcast had only moved his eyes twice. I thought to myself, "If he moved his eyes just two times, I'll read it with one movement, no problem."

"Okay, David," she said. "Your turn."

With the teacher's eyes locked onto mine, I stared at the line. How could I keep my eyes from moving? I first considered just staring at the page, but I was too scared I'd get caught, so I read the entire line, hoping that my eyes would not make a single unnecessary movement. Then I looked up. The verdict was about to be announced.

I held my breath, still anticipating that she'd say I read the line in one movement like the "smarter" kids (but I was prepared to settle for a worst-case scenario of two eye movements). She told the class that I had moved my eyes not once, or twice, but three times.

I was devastated. I insisted that something must be wrong. But the teacher would not change her mind. I had scored worse than any other student in the class.

I spent the rest of the day in mourning. Maybe I wasn't a very good reader. Perhaps I wasn't even intelligent. I was in a class for academically gifted students, yet somehow I no longer felt like I belonged.

It didn't take long for me to forget about the episode. The memory was too painful, so I suppressed it into my unconscious. But as it lodged in there, it had altered my personality and my self-perception. My confidence was replaced with a nagging doubt that I was just not good enough: I was not as gifted or as smart as the other students, so I lost the motivation to study. My grades in every class began to drop. I felt less confident in class and stopped interacting with the other students as I had before. I felt like I was not as good as them, and therefore I didn't think they would accept me.

Many years later, the unconscious memory lived on in my pursuits. Although I was an experienced orator, I would often listen to other well-known speakers and then redesign my message to imitate theirs. I felt that they were more accomplished than me, so what they had to say was somehow better than my own content. One traumatic moment (or at least one ego-shattering event) had redefined who I believed myself to be. And now it affected my career and shaped my dreams and pursuits.

Even when I began to achieve success, the memory lived on in my nonconscious mind. Any success I achieved was shadowed by doubts and even depression. I felt like a fraud when I did well because being a successful person wasn't who I believed myself to be unconsciously. Depression was a way to punish myself for the lack of harmony between the success I witnessed and how I felt about myself in my nonconscious mind.

A combination of guilt, shame, and fear had entrenched itself as the filters through which I viewed reality. I could not be happy with myself even when I did well. It wasn't that the incident in the classroom was the sole reason for my struggles. The unconscious negative programming had begun almost the moment I was born. But somehow the minor event in the classroom had a traumatic effect on me and intensified the disconnect from my *true self*. Although I was not consciously aware of it, my life was being shaped by one teacher's experiment.

All of us have different experiences that shape our sense of self. We are by-products of our upbringings and what we have experienced and learned in life. Those events live on as the stories we tell ourselves about who we are. Whether our understanding of what happened is factually correct or not doesn't matter, because what remains as an unconscious memory is our interpretation of what happened. Combined with other memories, these stories about who we are form an egoic pattern in our subconscious that then determines our conscious thought-patterns, beliefs, passions, and pursuits.

Unless we experience transformation, the underlying emotion is fear (whether we are aware of it or not). This fear shows up in a combination of ways, fluctuating from one moment to another as self-doubt or conceit, anxiety or arrogance, self-loathing or self-righteousness. But lurking below the surface is always an egoic struggle to be unique and superior to others. The inner unconscious anxiety that *I'm not enough* has become part of our identity. Unaware of our true essence, we are afraid of rejection and loneliness, scared that our lives won't matter, and worried (or indifferent) about what people think of us. Fear is the unrelenting and unconscious guide of our life, because the concept of *I* has entrenched itself so deeply in our mind that we have forgotten who we are.

To end the constant inner chatter of the ego that is the cause of the suffering in our mind, we need to regain awareness of the effervescent spirit of love—our *true self*—within us.

5

THE ILLUSION OF GOOD AND EVIL

I was only a toddler when I first became captivated with trees. Climbing trees was especially fascinating to me. If I could climb higher than my friends, it somehow made me feel unique. And for the first years of childhood, I was an unbeatable climber among my peers.

Until the dreadful day when I decided to use a branch of a tree as my airplane yoke. Picture the scene...

I'm straddling a big branch at the top of a tree, high above my friends on the ground. Suddenly, I'm a daring pilot making dangerous maneuvers through the sky as I steer the imaginary yoke to the left and right. Just as I start to make a hard-banking turn, I hear a crack. Suddenly, I'm back to being David "the unbeatable climber," and I'm in free fall through the air.

If I had a parachute, I'd pull the ripcord right now. But no such luck—I'm heading for a full-face collision with the ground.

With a scratched-up face, a broken nose, and a sprained wrist, I'm flat on the ground, crying for help. Fortunately, my dad comes to the rescue, and after a visit to the hospital, I'm told I'll be just fine. But not before the pediatrician tells me to leave the airplane flying to the professionals. Thanks, Doc.

I was lucky to only incur minor injuries, but I still learned a valuable lesson: when you get too cocky about your own abilities, you may experience a humiliating fall. In other words, the ego has an uncanny ability to get us all into trouble.

Much later in life I learned how trees throughout history have had a mysterious and at times symbolic connection with the ego. Buddhism, for example, finds its origin in the Buddha who spent 49 days of meditation under a fig tree. Later, that tree became known as the tree of enlightenment because it symbolized the place where Buddha experienced freedom from the sufferings of the egoic mind.

Trees also play a central role in the Bible, where they are woven throughout a narrative about humanity and its relationship with God. The tale of trees begins at the beginning of the first library of books that make up the Bible and sets the tone for everything that follows until the final text's culmination. So central are trees that without understanding their symbolism, the Bible gets distorted and misrepresented. As we have seen throughout history, the Bible can be used as a weapon of intolerance, inequality, bigotry, misogyny, racism, xenophobia and even war.

In Case You Wonder....

This may be a good time to share why I think the Bible is still worth reading. Because I get it: unless we are afraid to question what we read in the Bible (which is not uncommon in many church circles) most of us may at times find the Bible to be out of touch, confusing, and morally suspect. There's just a lot in the Bible that's weird.

That is not too surprising considering the Bible is an ancient book (or should I say a compilation of 66 ancient books) written over the course of 2000 years. The last book was written almost 2000 years ago —long before there were any satellites in space that could instantly transmit our latest opinions to the world through Facebook Live. So if we go to the Bible looking for the perfect "recipe" to follow in a culture where cable news, Twitter, or anything Kardashian is the daily diet, then we may just wonder if the Bible has anything to offer us today.

So what is the Bible? After decades of studying and teaching the Bible, I would suggest that it's not so much a history book (although there's much history in there). It's not really a theological discourse with rules to obey, either (even though there are many rules in there). It's a story about humanity's quest to understand the purpose of life by interacting with what they perceived to be God...in the time and place they lived.

And that's an important distinction, because a book that spans the writings of at least 40 writers over a period of 2000 years is bound to align with when and where the writers lived. In the early writings, God was a pretty vindictive, controlling, war-mongering figure, but then gets progressively nicer. Finally, by the end of the Bible, the descriptions turn passionately to *God is love* (and I doubt this progression has anything to do with God aging.) Even in the New Testament, which was supposedly written over the course of less than 50 years, the writers, often in conflict with each other, struggled to make sense of how the life of love that Jesus introduced should be expressed in their community and in the world.

So when you step back and observe the Bible from a broader view, what stands out above all is that over a period of two millennia, the Jewish writers' perception of God progressed—not always in a straight line—toward a more equitable and less tribal world.

That simple fact is perhaps a clue to how the Bible actually works. What I mean is that the message of the Bible is that it's okay to reimagine God as the world changes. The Bible helps us understand that we should not get stuck in traditions that divide and separate, but rather follow the trajectory of history toward a more inclusive world. From that perspective, the mysteries, plots, characters, struggles, and victories of the Bible are there to reflect upon, question, prod, and guide us toward a more unifying and compassionate Christ-centric consciousness. In fact, reading it any other way is actually unhealthy for the world we live in.

This may get me a lot of not-so-friendly emails, but I'm suggesting that when we look to the Bible for a set of thoughts (beliefs) that we consider the absolute truth rather than as a pathway to finding wisdom about love and oneness, we end up trapped under the spell of the ego, which desperately seeks approval and acceptance by the rightness of its religion.

Which brings me back to the importance of trees in the Bible. It seems to me that understanding the symbolism of trees can turn the Bible from an old and outdated set of books into mystical, majestic, and metaphorical literature written to open our hearts to the deepest parts within us. In fact, the two trees are central to understanding how humanity imagines God.

So how about we delve into the story of trees at the outset of Genesis to find out what a mystical narrative may communicate and unmask about the nature of the ego and the ways we experience reality...

The Trees in the Garden

We begin with the backdrop to the story, because otherwise this tale of trees in the Garden of Eden can be pretty depressing. Before the Hebrew writers (who had been slaves and were now in exile in Babylon) share the story of trees, they want future generations of Jewish people to know that in spite of what they had experienced, they believed in the goodness of humanity. They begin their story by saying that creation is inherently good, created in the image and likeness of God, who "breathes" the essence of divine life into visible matter, and makes man and woman living souls. And that is very good. But somehow a tree gets in the way and changes the course of their history.

Resembling narratives of other traditions, the Hebrew story of the Garden of Eden is about a talking snake, a man and a woman, a god who is out for a morning stroll in the woods, and (of course) two trees. The story seems bizarre, but as many myths told throughout history, it has a deeper meaning.

The names of the place and its characters were carefully chosen to communicate a more profound truth:

The Garden of Eden is probably a metaphorical reference to the hidden eternal dimension in us that are in union with God. The word *Eden* comes from the Hebrew word *ednah*, which means delight, pleasure, and is closely related to the words *eternal*, *moment*, and *presence*. Interestingly enough, the Hebrew term for heaven or paradise is in fact *Gan Eden*—meaning the Garden of Eden. When we think of heaven or paradise, we immediately assume it's an unknown location far removed from ours. But right here at the outset of the Bible, it seems to imply that heaven is not a geographically separate place from the earth, as much as a state of being. Paradise, heaven, and the Garden of Eden are cast as metaphorical expressions for being in a state of pure bliss, delight, and pleasure, where we are awake to the divine *presence* of love.

Adam and Eve. The name Adam means *man*, or *to be red*, and speaks to the physical and material aspects of humanity. The woman's name is Eve, and means *to breathe, to live,* or *to give life*, and refers to the spiritual. The names communicate the inexplicable connectedness of matter and spirit that results in a living being.

As the story is told, life for Adam begins in paradise in union with God. A body is formed from the dust of the ground, representing the earthly nature of humanity, and what we know today as visible matter. Similar to the chair you are sitting in, or the book or device you are holding in your hand, the body was lifeless ordinary matter until God breathed spirit—the essence of divine being—into humanity and Adam became a living being or a soul.

The subtlety of an allegorical interpretation of the text communicates the quintessence of life. To be human is to inhabit visible matter with all its limitations, while simultaneously being imbued with the divine spirit that knows no limits. The mind can identify with ordinary matter that points out the separation, or it can identify with spirit, which means being aware of the *presence* of the divine, and our unity with all. When we identify with the separation—the ego—it ultimately leads to pain and suffering; while identifying with spirit creates a mindset of bliss in paradise.

According to the story, Adam and Eve enjoyed their extraordinary union with God. While inhabiting distinct physical bodies, they must have perceived their oneness because their sensory perception was based on spirit rather than the physical elements. They were as one, naked and not ashamed because they enjoyed a blissful awareness of God (Love).

Nudity in this allegory was not so much a physical condition, but instead an allusion to being completely exposed, where nothing within was hidden. Everything was in the open, and Adam and Eve were not ashamed. While guilt is an emotion that suggests I have done something wrong, shame is a feeling of fear that communicates that there is something wrong with me. Being ashamed speaks to our sense of identity as not being enough the way we are. Although Adam and Eve were uncovered entirely, they didn't identify with their bodies. Maybe because they were one in spirit with one another and God, and therefore their physical separation (and how they related to it) was inconsequential. They identified with *spirit*—the energy of love that unites everything—and consequently, were sentient or conscious of the *presence*.

The underlying message in the story appears obvious. To be completely naked—where our inner world is known—without a feeling of shame is plausible when we are intimately aware of our oneness with God and the unifying divine love that we participate in and are part of.

Up until now, this story—which is rich with allegory about the essence of being—is clear. Our happiness, health, and success spring from mindfulness of our union with one another and the divine. In this union, there's no separation because we are all one in love.

The Deception of Separation

Out of nowhere there suddenly appears a talking serpent. The Hebrew etymology for serpent signifies *twist* or *spin* and stems from an onomatopoetic (coming soon to a spelling bee near you) word for *hiss* or *whisper*. It suggests a twisting, spinning, or moving whisper, and later became the word for *enchanter*. If you have ever been around a chronic liar, you know the concept being referenced. A habitual liar tells stories that are continually evolving and moving in subtleties and plausible fabrications. Listening to his voice is like being under a spell, where we are charmed to see the world as he sees it. The deceptive spell and the hissing whisper in this story was the ego's formation in our mind.

When we were first born, we enjoyed the blissful innocence of life. At some point, probably between the ages of one or two, we became increasingly conscious of the concept of self, or *I*. The ego was formed and began to look for significance, value, and love outside itself. It needed a path to find it, and the world of duality was introduced.

The story of beginnings refers to this polarizing duality as the tree of knowledge of good and evil that brought with it death. Death here is not about annihilation or a physical end to life, for the word merely means *separation*. Eating the fruit of the tree of knowledge of good and evil would alienate the mind from the divine spirit. They would no longer be conscious of their oneness with the divine *being*. The separation was not real, but an illusion invented by the mind. Yet the perceived separation would have consequences, as we see in the story.

The tree's emphasis on knowledge of good and evil is deliberate. Gaining knowledge implies being able to learn something and store it in your memory. The word *knowledge* also meant *to perceive, discriminate, judge,* and *to know by experience*.

So what was the tree of knowledge of good and evil?

It was a value system that gave Adam and Eve the ability to *judge* good from evil, right from wrong. Of course, isn't the ability to discern good from evil a wonderful quality? After all, what would the world be like without a value system that defines right from wrong? I agree. It makes sense.

Except the value system has a major flaw.

The ability to *perceive* good from evil in self was based on whether one experienced guilt or not. Guilt and love can, of course, never co-exist. When we experience guilt, we are essentially saying that we are not worthy of unconditional love. So gaining knowledge of good and evil without first eating the fruit of the tree of life separated Adam and Eve from awareness of God as love. Guilt demanded that they become good enough to earn love and acceptance, which resulted in shame—the feeling that *I am not enough the way I am*. In other words, they were no longer conscious of their *true self*.

Unaware of God, each person became the center of their own world, and just like that, selfishness was born. Whatever was good was now determined in the absence of awareness of love. Good became defined by the egoic conscience seared in guilt that sought to preserve its sense of self, and longed for recognition, approval, and significance by how it stood out from others.

So here is how it played out. The instant they gained knowledge of good and evil, they were able to discern what was good for self, but they were unable to comprehend how this knowledge applied to "others." Their understanding of good was limited to their own personal interest.

We can observe this same fallacy of knowledge of good and evil even today. Why does a person lie, steal, or commit adultery? Because at the moment, he sees it as beneficial to himself. Lying or stealing at the time seems good for him. He fails to see the bigger picture based on the unifying *presence* of love, and doesn't consider the effects his actions will have on the other person involved. It's good for him, even though it is evil to another. Of course, most people may not be unfaithful, or engage in illegal activites. Yet it doesn't take long to detect selfishness in the heart of humanity. There are even times when our cares and concerns for others are rooted in the ego's quest for love and acceptance by way of what we do for others.

How The Tree Impacts You Today

What can you learn from this story about the tree of knowledge of good and evil?

First, *the tree is a symbol of how you perceive yourself and experience the world.*

The tree of knowledge of good and evil represents an illusionary unconscious perception in your mind. You view reality through the prism of good and evil, and therefore cannot perceive the union that you share with all.

Second, *the mindset of knowledge of good and evil raised in this story is the cause of the divisions in the world, and is the enemy of oneness and love.*

It doesn't take long for us to see the effects of knowledge of good and evil in the world today. Religion, which is often the most prevalent and ostentatious definer of good and evil, is the cause of so much division (and even hatred) in the world. The concept of good and evil is also commonly promulgated by politicians to place themselves on the right side and their opponents on the wrong side of issues and character. The end result is further division that, at times, leads to conflict and even war.

Then there are also more subtle subconscious ways by which we define good and evil. A career as a physician, lawyer, teacher, and so on may be the "good" that the ego pursues. Others seek fame or fortune to validate their existence to somehow become "good" enough for love, acceptance, and approval. These judgments further separate people, often unconsciously, into various levels of who is good and who is not. In other words, it opposes a transcending reality rooted in oneness and love.

Third, *the story describes how the formation of the ego resulted in a distorted view of God, where the* INFINITE *is made in the likeness and image of the false self.*

The ego, taking its cues from the five senses, is obviously not able to discern the spiritual embodiment of the divine in the universe. So it projects its own limited knowledge and inferior wisdom on that which transcends all, and imagines a God that is an object among an endless number of objects—all separated by time and space. Of course, this God is the most powerful of all beings—and a male, too, because the man is stronger than the woman (must have been a male ego). *He* is resting in his heavenly home, seated on his throne, far removed from the ungodly Earth. Superior to all other beings, this god is the ultimate judge of what is good and evil.

I admit that I'm generalizing a bit here, but think about it: the way that most religions speak about God is quite primitive, especially in light of what we now know about the universe. While God may no longer be portrayed as some alien going for early morning walks in the forest, God is often referred to with male pronouns as sitting far away upstairs on his throne (I assume in some galactic palace beyond the universe). He, like Santa Claus, is watching carefully to see whether we have been good or bad. Beyond the slight hint of sarcasm here, the reality is that we see a version of this perception of God played out every week in many churches across the United States (and in many other parts of the world).

As long as the ego continues to serve as the unconscious perception of people, we cannot help but project our need for significance and power onto God. Unaware of that dimension within us that is one with love, we want a strong, powerful, judgmental God that is for me and against others. To quiet the nagging feeling that we are not enough for love, I need a God that's on my side and opposes my enemies.

The Consequences of Separation

Once Adam and Eve ate the fruit of the tree of knowledge of good and evil, the separation was almost complete. A shift of consciousness had occurred. Awareness of spirit had turned to intellectual reasoning based on the five senses. The transference from the *love-union* consciousness to the *fear-self* perception would have an immediate impact.

It began with *shame.* Adam and Eve suddenly noticed their nakedness and made clothes out of fig leaves to cover up. What else could be expected? When you perceive myself as separate, it summons fear that you may not be good enough. The mind, at least subconsciously, may conclude:

"Don't let anyone see your failures, weaknesses, and insecurities. You are naked and need something to hide behind. Find something that will make you appear special and superior to others. That way you will stand out in the crowd."

With shame came *fear* in the Garden of Eden. God was walking in the Garden, and Adam and Eve hid among the trees, for they were afraid of God. The ego is always terrified of being exposed, humiliated, and disapproved of. It fears the judge, *our conscience*, and the hell of inner torment and suffering that awaits as punishment for our wrongdoings. It's afraid of anything that threatens its carefully crafted identity. Most of all, it fears death—the end of its importance.

In the hope of avoiding judgment, we hide behind work, alcohol, drugs, food, and any other compulsions that make us forget for a moment our failures, weaknesses, and insecurities. But the judge, our conscience, always re-appears in the restlessness of the night, and in those moments when we are alone with only our thoughts. The verdict is still the same. You are not enough for love, and punishment is required.

While consciously we may be unaware of the sentencing we have received, the hell that we live in demonstrates this unconscious conviction. Stress, anxiety, and unhappiness are just some of the punishment levied by our subconscious. We have sent ourselves to hell—a place of inner torment within us. Imprisoned by our thoughts, we don't know how to escape the pain and suffering of the hell that we have created.

Every infraction, every misdeed, and every failure has its own unique sentence. If we get fired from our job, and the list of excuses runs out, we turn the finger on ourselves. We are guilty, and now the shame of not being enough the way we are demands some form of punishment. Whether it is depression, sickness, poverty, or even divorce, our subconscious knows how to inflict the type of punishment we believe we deserve. Eating the fruit of the tree of knowledge of good and evil has become our way of life.

I shared earlier about the cluster headaches that I suffered when I first moved to California. Looking back, I recognize the guilt I felt. I had failed and felt unworthy. Unable to hide behind my success, I subconsciously sent myself to the hell of excruciating cluster headaches. The pain was my subconscious self-inflicted punishment, and its purpose was to alleviate the guilt. I needed to feel that I had paid for my sins, which would help me be free. At least, that was the reasoning of the ego deep in my subconscious.

By now you may wonder, "What good is it to know what's wrong in our life if this egoic mindset is so pervasive and destructive? Why even bring it up if there's no credible path out of our suffering?" The reason is quite simple: the return to divine love for most of us begins in moments of darkness. By observing the darkness within you and actually accepting it for what it is, you allow the ego to loosen its control, and you surrender to the light of grace. The point, therefore, is to expose the darkness, because it is only then that your heart is more likely to be receptive to the light of love.

Returning to the story about the Garden of Eden: we find Adam and Eve were confronted with their failures. It didn't take but a moment for Adam to throw Eve under the bus. (Some things never change, right?) "The woman you gave me is to blame," he told God. Adam's line of defense was clear: *I'm a victim. It's not my fault. It's Eve's fault, and it's your fault because you gave her to me.*

The mind under the spell of the ego has an amazing capacity to shift responsibility away from itself. When the ego is being threatened, the false self points the finger at anything outside the conceptualized self, and without hesitation retreats into a shell of victimhood.

For example, as children, when we were confronted by our parents for something we did wrong, we blamed our brother, sister, teacher, neighbor, cat, dog and even our parents—because it's never *my* fault as far as the ego is concerned. As we have seen, to accept responsibility is to admit guilt. And guilt means punishment, and punishment involves pain, and pain is the prelude to death.

The story of the trees ends with Adam and Eve being shut out of the Garden of Eden. The Garden had to be preserved because only then could it remain the place of bliss, pleasure, and delight. At some point, when the fruit of the tree of knowledge of good and evil had lost its appeal, there would appear light to illuminate a path back to paradise—the hidden eternal dimension within us that's one with the divine essence of love.

The story of the Garden of Eden and the tree of knowledge of good and evil set the tone for the rest of the Bible. Every person who interacts with God in this sacred text views materiality through the prism of the tree of illusion until Jesus comes on the scene with a radically different view of reality. Contrary to every instinct of the ego, Jesus speaks of love for our enemies, doing good to those who hate us, serving one another, and laying down our lives for others. The ultimate expression of Jesus' egoless archetype was his death on a tree, signifying the self-less nature of divine love, followed by his resurrection, representing the power of divine love over death.

We have not discussed the tree of life, which was mentioned in the story of trees in the Garden of Eden. For now, I'll say this: the cross is symbolic of the tree of life. The deeper meaning of Jesus' death on a tree speaks to the death of the ego, where our ego (guilt, shame, fear) or *I* is crucified with Christ. The resurrection is then the awakened life where identifying with form has come to an end, and where again we identify with spirit and our eternal formless love-union with all things.

So yes, by now you may understand why I was so captivated by trees as a child. As symbols in the Bible, they are filled with deep meaning, both in the form of the tree of life, and the tree of knowledge of good and evil. As playgrounds for the imagination, they offer infinite possibilities. But take my word for it: don't let your ego turn a tree into a vehicle for arrogance—such as, I don't know, an airplane. I should know. I have the childhood scars to prove it.

6

THE QUEST OF THE EGO

Now, after talking about a garden, a couple of trees, and their relation to our ego, let's explore the ways the ego creates unhappiness, unhealthy relationships, and even sickness.

The ego is on a quest. It needs to feel special and stand out among its peers. Therefore, the ego looks for ways to be superior to others as a means to cope with the inner loneliness and aching subconscious feeling that *I'm not good enough the way I am*. By establishing lack in someone else, and boasting about its own value, the ego is strengthened and concludes its own unique superiority.

The early years of life determine many of the pursuits of the ego. Family, tradition, religion, and culture all influence our perception of what we consider the highest good. While family, tradition, and religion play important roles in determining how the ego pursues its own uniqueness and specialness, culture also has a huge influence on selfhood. Here in the United States (and in many of the most prosperous nations), the culture lends itself to ranking people based on net worth, power, and fame. Inherent in the collective psyche is, therefore, an ambition to succeed on Wall Street or in Hollywood, seek power through what we call higher office, or attain recognition and applause through sports or music.

I'm not suggesting that everyone who runs for office, uses their talents on the big screen, or is engaged in any other high-profile dream is any more under the ego's grip than someone who works at the local animal shelter. Ultimately, it's not the nature of what we pursue that matters, but rather the motivation behind it that determines whether it will lead to suffering or peace. What I mean is that the ego pursues whatever validates and strengthens its sense of self — a pursuit that ultimately ends in suffering. On the other hand, love takes the gifts and talents that we have and expresses them in ways that bring others and ourselves joy and wholeness. The point here, of course, is that culture has a pull on the ego, especially wherever culture serves a prominent role within the family structure, or where there is lack of affirmation, approval, and acceptance by parents or the systems in which we are raised.

Ultimately, whatever the ego pursues in an effort to gain the upper hand over others comes at a price. Specialness opposes oneness and oneness is the ultimate design of love. The more we yield to the ego, therefore, the more we suffer from pain, conflict, and unrest. When our sense of identity is based on the ego's achievement and success (or lack thereof), it moves us further away from awareness of the unconditional love that holds us all together.

On the other hand, when your identity is established in the union of love, then your talents and abilities become expressions of the divine in the world. From that perspective, you are no longer looking for prominence, but instead you seek to participate in the union that we all share together. Your gifts and skills are then used to bring the beauty of life to the world around you.

Let's look at a few examples from everyday life as an illustration of how the ego seeks out ways to be unique and superior.

Identifying with Physical Appearance

Almost every day I go for a hike or a run for 40 or more minutes in my neighborhood. Although the weather is usually quite warm even in the wintertime here in San Diego, the daytime temperature drops into the 40s a few times every year. In that brisk cold air, I wear warm workout clothes, including a hoody over my head, and a pair of sunglasses to shield against the glare of the sun. (One time, a friend suggested that my cold weather outfit makes me look like the Unabomber. That's not the look I'm going for, but nevertheless, you get the picture: I'm covered up when it's cold outside.)

On one such cold California day, a fellow runner passed me, and I noticed he was wearing shorts and no shirt. His attire seemed a bit outrageous, but when I saw his bulking physique and how the people inside the passing cars seemed unable to look away, I couldn't help but wonder if there was something more going on. What's undeniable is that to varying degrees, most of us identify with our bodies, whether that's our looks, the clothes we wear, or our level of fitness.

That body identification raises a question: What happens when age creeps up on us, and people stop admiring our good looks, or when we cannot afford new designer clothes because we lost our job, or our Instagram following is upended by a younger influencer, or when cosmetic surgery goes wrong, and we are left to handle the terrifying humiliation? Pain and anguish await anyone whose self-identity is based on their appearance, because age and bad breaks have a way of catching up to us all.

Undoubtedly, it's good to take care of our bodies. To work out is good for our health, and to completely disregard our appearance can be a sign of mental health issues. Besides, when we present ourselves well, we are honoring others, in a way: care for our body is a symbol of love.

But when our physical appearance is tied to self-worth and self-identity, we will inevitably experience suffering at some point. If our self-identity rests mostly in our looks, then our conceptualized selfhood will be strengthened only as long as we get compliments and validation from others. The moment we're made to feel insecure about our appearance, we'll inevitably experience some form of emotional letdown or crisis. We may become anxious, irritated, or depressed, or we may lash out at the "haters." When hurt, the ego needs to find someone or something outside its perceived self to criticize and judge.

By redirecting fault away from self, the ego tries to cover up the nagging doubt that *I'm not enough the way I am*. Yet the root problem remains: our self-identity is based on physical appearance rather than on spirit. When we base our identity on our image, we give more credence to the validation and approval we get from others, rather than the profound inward witness of the *spirit* that is in union with the *divine*.

The Need to Be Right

The lease on my car was almost up, so I swung by the dealership to see what they could offer me. I needed a good deal to get a win and feel special. (Remember: the ego likes to win because it perceives winning as strength.)

When I pulled into the dealership, I was greeted by the same sixty-something-year-old man who sold me the car I was driving.

Although his name revealed a similar Scandinavian background to mine, his demeanor and attire communicated our differences.

"What do you think of your TLX?" he said.

I had bought the car from him a couple of years before, and I'm sure he expected a favorable response as I had returned looking for a new vehicle from his dealership.

With a slight hesitation in my voice, I said, "I like the car, I do, but the voice command feature of the GPS is a bit disappointing."

He seemed taken aback. "That's strange. I haven't heard that before." Implied in his answer was that I was the only one having the problem, and therefore the mistake was probably mine.

Whenever we are in a conversation with someone, there is a subliminal communication happening in concurrence with our verbal exchange. Our conscious mind operates at a much slower rate than the subconscious. We may not be able to articulate what's happening, but unconsciously we pick up on the other person's energy. In the case of the car dealer, the ego perceived a threat. My subconscious heard that "You are the only one with this problem, so it must be your fault. You are not smart enough to figure out how to make the GPS work."

The first egoic-instinct when you feel attacked is to defend yourself. I remembered comments that I heard from several others, including another person involved with the same dealership, that my issue with the GPS was a common complaint. But whether it was my desire for a good deal or just a moment of restraint, I decided to say nothing. Instead, I thanked him and proceeded to back out of the parking lot.

Just as I was leaving, the sales rep motioned for me to roll down my window. I stopped to hear what he had to say. Clearing his throat, he looked at me and asked, "What did you mean about the GPS not working very well?"

"Let me show you," I responded.

While the salesperson leaned in through my side window, I proceeded to use the voice command feature of the GPS. With clear and slow speech for emphasis, I gave instructions to the GPS to take me to an address in La Jolla, California, about 20 minutes away from the dealership. After a few moments of searching, the GPS revealed an address in Idaho, more than 2,000 miles northeast. With a sense of validation and self-satisfaction, I looked at him and "casually" said, "You see what I'm talking about?"

Suddenly, he became quite defensive and asked me to get out of the car so he could try it for himself. When I declined, he muttered something about my accent possibly being the reason why the GPS was not locating the correct address.

"My accent?!" I thought to myself. I was born in Sweden, but I have lived most of my life in Canada and the US. I may have a slight accent, but I speak publicly in various forums, and know how to speak clearly.

So I looked him in the eyes, and with a firm voice reverted to my self-ascribed lawyerly defense.

"Are you telling me that Acura doesn't make cars for people with my accent? Or are you telling me that Acura is not capable of making cars for people like me? Or are you suggesting that Acura doesn't *want* customers who, like me, are immigrants to this nation?"

For a moment, I felt really good. With just three short questions, I had managed to make it an immigration issue, while at the same time implying that Acura was an inferior carmaker. Seeing the bewildered look in the salesperson's eyes, I reached out my hand and told him, "No hard feelings. Unfortunately, I have to leave. Thank you for your time."

Driving away, I spent the first minute fluctuating between anger at the rudeness of the sales rep and guilt about my irritated response. But then the whole episode crystalized into clarity. The entire exchange was nothing more than the ego rearing its ugly head.

I had interpreted his comments as an attack on my identity. Struggling with the inescapable feeling that *I may not be enough the way I am*, the conversation had fueled my insecurities. Derogatory comments that I heard when I first came to Canada and didn't speak much English lived on decades later in my subconscious. And somehow I also felt less about myself because I was an immigrant. Becoming a US citizen was a long and, at times, debasing process, and its aftereffect was still lingering deep inside me.

So my response was the ego's counter-attack. I needed to win the argument for my self-worth to return. By turning it into an immigration issue and a criticism of the carmaker, I made myself a victim and my opponent a heartless salesperson who didn't care for people like me. I had also "successfully" argued my point and caused my opponent to become defensive and speechless, hence my feeling of superiority about my intelligence level and debating skills. I had reversed a loss into a win and had reason to celebrate.

Except…

The whole incident was nothing more than a pointless battle of egos.

To validate my sense of identity, I needed to be right, and I needed my opponent to be wrong. What purpose did that achieve? Did I walk away with a new car? Did I leave with a good feeling? By the end, I had lost both time and energy. My mind was stuck reliving the incident in a stream of negativity and judgment, when it could have been engaged in something uplifting. I had turned the salesperson into an enemy rather than a friend, and thus failed to recognize the divine union we share.

Moments like this one, where the ego seeks to strengthen its worth, repeat themselves over and over again in life. When multiplied, these incidents form unconscious programming that can lead to all kinds of anxieties and even sicknesses. Scientific studies suggest that experiences do not just reside in our brains, but are recorded at the cellular level throughout our bodies. These cellular memories are the source of most of our illness and disease. One example is cancer. Showing up in our bodies later in life, the cancer may be due to stress or fear related to memories programmed into our cells at an earlier age.

The good news is that these cellular memories that have forgotten how to be healthy can be manipulated to return to a state of peace. Studies show that unconditional love has a profound effect on our cells. We can recode our cells by reprogramming our subconscious with love; thus transforming our sense of identity, healing our cellular memories, and improving our health and wellbeing.

Complaining and the Role of the Victim

When feelings of unworthiness and failure are etched in the subconscious, the ego creates another false self that we commonly refer to as the victim. "People are against me, and I get no breaks" becomes our inner dialogue. This type of reasoning creates a form of delusional superiority. "No one has experienced what I have. No one has suffered like me. No one has been betrayed to the degree that I have." We feel special in our failures, thus strengthening our self-imposed identity as a victim.

The most common way the ego fortifies its role as a victim is by complaining, whether in the mind or out loud. We complain about where we are, who we are with, what we are doing but don't want to do, what happened to us that should not have happened, what didn't happen to us that should have happened, or how people wronged us. When the ego perceives a threat against itself, it reverts to the role of victim, and will then find something to complain about.

Sometimes we can get trapped in a complaining pattern, where even the most minuscule issues are judged. You could be reading this book outside in your backyard, and suddenly your neighbor begins to mow their lawn and you could complain to yourself, "Every time I sit down for some peace and quiet someone interrupts it. I just knew it would happen. It never fails."

Whatever you complain about you are making into your enemy. This reinforces your mind's perceived separation from the all-encompassing oneness of the divine. Unaware of the love that permeates the universe, we seek solace in the role of a victim. Viewing ourselves as persecuted makes us feel oddly heroic. We were wronged, and complaining becomes our way of executing justice.

The nature of the complaint is often associated with the petty frustrations that we experience every day. If we are at a restaurant and we get served cold pizza with less cheese and toppings than the other guests, the ego may take it as a personal attack. So we may confront the waiter in a way that establishes him and the restaurant as our adversary. We were *wronged* because *they* mistreated us. Complaining about being served a cold pizza, therefore, is the ego's attempt to regain its own worth by establishing the lack of worth in the other. "This is the second time I have been served cold pizza at this restaurant. Why would you bring me a cold pizza? This is terrible service. I don't deserve to be treated this way. I demand that you make me a new pizza, and I refuse to pay for it."

Airing our grievances in this manner fortifies the ego's sense of identity as a victim. We feel morally superior to them, and that makes us feel closer to the good of the god of our own making.

Now I'm not suggesting that a person takes on the form of a martyr and does nothing when they are wronged, because that would be just another device of the ego to bolster its perception of being a victim. For instance, victims of abuse should not make excuses for destructive or degrading treatment by others. Often the most appropriate step of love is to leave the abuser and report the person to the authorities in an effort to minimize future abusive behavior.

And in the case of the cold pizza, you can speak to the waiter in a way that avoids making the issue about good or evil. Without a negative and accusatory tone, you can say to the waiter, "Excuse me, but my pizza is cold. Is it possible to get it heated or remade?" And then thank them for their help. From that position, you are not making the waiter your foe as a means to fortify your illusionary ego, nor are you cultivating the ego's role as victim. Instead, you are allowing a grateful attitude to solidify the union you share with the waiter.

Being grateful, then, is a way to stop arguing with what is, and remain in a place of inner happiness. When you complain, you poison your state of consciousness with unhappiness. The ego associates victimization with sadness. The subconscious makes the case that "I have the right to be unhappy because I have been wronged." But when you remain in gratitude, you refuse to give in to the ego's victimization. It's there that you will experience inner (and contagious) happiness that paves the way for good things to happen.

One time, I was scheduled on a flight from Europe to Los Angeles. Arriving early at the airport, I asked the check-in staff if I could use my points to upgrade to a flatbed seat in Premier Business Class. The representative assured me that it was possible, but I would need to visit the sales office in another section of the airport. So I went there and was yet again referred to another sales office on the gate side of the terminal.

Passing through security, I arrived there about 20 minutes later. After a wait in line, I finally sat down with the representative and again asked if I could purchase an upgrade using my points. The agent looked at her computer and told me that she had two seats remaining, and would be delighted to help me. A few minutes passed while she was busy speaking to someone on the phone. Then she asked me for my credit card and the frequent flier account to charge for the upgrade. A few more minutes went by, and now she looked at me with a hint of distress and said, "I'm so sorry, sir, but someone else just purchased the last two Business Premier Class seats."

My mind could have easily raced toward the injustice of the situation. I had experienced one delay after another by what appeared to be an inattentive staff. Besides, I enjoyed my "special" status as a Platinum Frequent Flier member and a Million-Mile Flier. Now, I'd have to suffer the consequences of stuffing my 6-foot-5 frame into a small economy seat, because I couldn't upgrade my ticket. There was no shortage of arguments I could make to justify outrage for how the situation had been handled.

But rather than complaining, which would strengthen the ego's victim role, I expressed gratitude to the sales agent, who was already apologizing profusely. I told her not to worry about it, and reached out to shake her hand in appreciation. Again, she said how sorry she was, but unfortunately there were no more flatbed seats available on the flight. I felt her genuine embarrassment and identified with it. So I sincerely wished her all the best and walked away in an unusual state of calm. I realized that my level of comfort on the plane might be affected, but my happiness does not depend upon which seat I occupy.

About 30 minutes later, I arrived by the gate. As the flight was boarding, I suddenly heard my name being called to the gate desk. Approaching the counter, the woman working the desk handed me a new boarding pass in the Premier Business Class section. Moments later, I'm enjoying a flatbed seat without paying anything extra or using any of my frequent flier points.

Traveling 40,000 feet above the ground, I had the opportunity to reflect on the disadvantages of complaining and the benefits of gratefulness. I'm sure if I had complained, the sales agents would not have sought to pull any favors for me. But by accepting reality for what it is with an attitude of thankfulness, a portal of unexpected blessings and favor had opened up. I got to enjoy greater comfort for the 11-hour flight. When we remain in gratitude, we remain aware of love, where things have a way of working together for good.

While the ego is never content with now, and thus complains, gratitude is, in fact, the language of love that keeps you at peace with what is. So express heartfelt gratitude for life next time something or someone attempts to steal your joy. A continued attitude of gratitude will shift your consciousness away from the ego's pursuits, the trauma of the moment, and the feelings of insecurity and fear. Your focus will instead turn toward the beauty and the generosity of life, and the surpassing love and peace that is somehow woven into the fabric of the universe.

7

THE MYTH OF FAILURE

Nothing in the human experience is more universal than failure. The ways we fail vary, and some of our slip-ups are more serious than others. But almost every day, and often many times throughout the day, we make mistakes.

When we err, the primary emotion that we experience is guilt (for our behavior), followed by shame (relative to our identity). While both guilt and shame are destructive emotions, people sometimes confuse guilt with what I like to call *love's prompting*. If you offend someone, then *love's prompting* can cause you to make amends. This is a prompting by the *spirit* that is always void of judgment against self or others. Guilt, on the other hand, is embedded in fear and always leads to shame. It opposes and attacks universal love. Since the feeling of not being worthy of unconditional love is inherent in guilt, it turns into a profoundly destructive feeling of shame. Whereas love's prompting is an instructive voice of forgiveness and restoration.

Let's look at this story about Caitlin as an example. While

attending her best friend's bachelorette party in Miami, Caitlin got drunk and wound up having a public sexual encounter with a male stripper. When Caitlin told her husband, Alex, about what happened, he was at first disappointed, then moved past that feeling and forgave her. Caitlin, on the other hand, could not let it go. What she had done was so unlike her, and now her mind was consumed with what had happened.

"I feel so dirty, so guilty, and so filled with self-loathing," Caitlin told herself. "When I think about what I did, I'm disgusted with myself. I just want to throw up. The shame and guilt are ruining my life, my career, and my marriage. I'm filthy. I'm a cheater and cannot stand to look at myself in the mirror."

After 3 years of constantly reliving her past indiscretion and interpreting her reasons for the actions, Caitlin began to drink alcohol excessively as a way to escape the nagging guilt she felt every day. Eventually, Caitlin divorced Alex and started to engage in casual sex with married men at her workplace. Two years later she lost her job, and her health was deteriorating. Hitting rock bottom, Caitlin reached out for help and was eventually guided back to wholeness and health. Caitlin then remarried and found freedom, happiness, and wholeness as she awakened to her *true self*.

I share this story because guilt has a way of destroying us from the inside out. What can we learn about guilt from this story? To start, there is a difference between an event in our life and the story we tell ourselves about the event (guilt). The incident itself happened, but it was over almost as soon as it began. Once it was in the past, it was non-existent. But the story of the event lived on. Finding the answers to *Why?*, *What does it mean?*, and *What does that mistake say about me?* became an obsession in Caitlin's mind.

So what created the suffering and the anguish for Caitlin? Was it the event itself or the guilt-ridden story she kept telling herself? Of course it was the story (or her personal interpretation of what the incident meant) that created her suffering.

A story of an event is a mental construct in your mind consisting of words and images of events and characters. Something happens to you, and now the mind molds that event into a story that you repeat to yourself. The longer you tell that story, the more embellished, dramatic, and significant the event becomes. There are many different types of stories, but perhaps the most personally destructive ones are the stories of guilt.

So What Is Guilt?

Guilt is a fearful feeling that arises when we compromise or violate either a universal or personal moral code or rule.

Universal (or social) rules involve acceptable codes of conduct within a group, religion, culture, or society. These rules vary from one system to another, and will even change over time. What was unacceptable to our parents may be okay to us today. Breaking universal rules leads to guilt that requires some form of punishment imposed by the group, such as serving jail time or being shunned or shamed by the group.

Personal rules are individual beliefs about what you consider right and wrong, what your values are, and what is acceptable and unacceptable to you. Examples of personal rules range from what you are supposed to wear or what kind of people you should associate with, to how much quality time you spend with your kids. It involves anything that you have subconsciously agreed to as a personal code of conduct. Often your personal rules are shaped by the collective beliefs of your family, friends, and culture and formed in your mind at an early age.

When you break a personal rule, there is no police officer to arrest you, or social group to shame you. Therefore you experience emotional guilt that requires some form of punishment. As we discussed earlier, that punishment is imposed by the ego in your subconscious. Some of the most common kinds of egoic consequences are fearful self-destructive thoughts such as guilt, anxiety, depression, worry, and self-loathing. These negative emotions lead to addictions, sicknesses, and even premature death when allowed to fester in the subconscious.

How Guilt Affects Our Self-identity

Guilt is the self-defining voice of the ego. Since we identify with the ego, we innately believe that whatever we are feeling guilty about is who we are. Caitlin, for example, experienced extreme guilt from her initial sexual indiscretion. It was the first time she violated her personal rule, but the story lived on in her memory. At some point, the ego defined her subconsciously as a "filthy immoral cheater." The story she told herself about the event had altered her sense of identity. When we fail to live up to our standard of moral conduct, we feel guilty. That guilt is then embedded in our subconscious and contributes to our sense of identity. We are "bad," so we act out who we believe ourselves to be, such as an alcoholic or a cheater.

Yet without the guilty story that the egoic mind creates, the self-destructive behavior would never be able to establish itself as part of our identity. The fearful thought of guilt hooks us emotionally. That emotion moves us away from our *true self*. It separates us from awareness of love. The event may be real, but it is not lasting. The story about the fact, however, lives on in our memory and leads us to form false conclusions about who we are. In the case of Caitlin, she could not perceive herself as a spirit of love that's in union with God, her husband, and her family. Filled with self-hatred, she could not accept forgiveness, because the guilty story she told herself made her unlovable in her mind.

Where Guilt Begins...

So where do we learn our beliefs about guilt?

Think about it...

We instinctively believe that guilt is a call for punishment for the mistakes we make. Somehow we think that our self-imposed sentence will ease the pain of the guilt because enduring the punishment transforms us from bad to good people again. The truth is that guilt is a device created by the ego. It's the ego's self-correction and self-improvement strategy based on the fallacy that punishment leads to good behavior and that in turn makes us good people.

The ego adopts this guilt strategy at an early age. Perhaps it began when we got too excited and playful as children. Our parents, who were stressed after a long day at work, became irritated and angry with us. So they sent us to our room for a while, or worse they were demeaning toward us and even used physical force to carry out the punishment for our enthusiasm.

Each time events like this are played out in our childhood, a debilitating encoding occurs in our subconscious. There are good and evil behaviors, and there are right and wrong behaviors. When we do wrong, we are guilty and therefore bad. Bad people must be punished because it's only then they will learn to be good.

When Alex forgave Caitlin and encouraged her to move on from the event, she couldn't because her subconscious falsely believed that only after she was punished enough for her offense, then she would be a better person.

So guilt is really an attack on love, used by the ego to strengthen itself. The ego doesn't want to surrender to love, because it would mean the end to the reign of the ego. Caitlin could not receive love or become aware of love, because the ego would not allow it. The guilt ensured the continuity of the ego's reign.

What's more, the way of love seems like an erroneous deception to the ego. It reasons that unconditional and selfless love cannot be the answer to what's wrong in me or the world. So the ego opposes love through its guilt strategy.

But when you wake up to your true essence of love, that love permeates your subconscious and transforms your mind. The fear and guilt moral compass is replaced with awareness of selfless love that now effortlessly guides your actions, thoughts, and attitudes. You act out who you believe yourself to be. Your subconscious pervades with selfless unifying love, and therefore your instincts, actions, desires, and even passions reflect that love.

In the case of Caitlin, when she awakened to the spirit of love, she was able to forgive and let go of her past. It was only then that she experienced newfound happiness and wholeness. Caitlin was able to remarry and start a family because her sense of identity had been transformed.

How Religion Has Missed the Mark

If you were raised in the church, like me, then you are familiar with sin and its association with guilt. Sin was essentially a label attached to anything we did that was deemed wrong, immoral, or evil. God hates sin, we were told, and is quick to banish us to Hell for eternity for even the smallest thing we do wrong. But we can escape Hell if we ask for forgiveness from our sin, and then repent and obey the laws of God to become a better person. I want to state that this view about sin is not a universally accepted Christian doctrine. Many also view sin as *missing the mark* to who we are —unaware of our union with the *whole*. Nevertheless, a large segment of Christianity, especially in the United States, adheres to a more punishing narrative of the meaning of sin.

Not surprisingly, obeying the law (or the rules) to become a better person is the ego's interpretation of the story of the Bible. It's the ego's answer to the problem of evil and what's wrong in the world. But its message is flawed because it reasons that *I* (or the ego) can be reformed and saved. The ego wants to be reformed and saved from the evil impulses it developed in its unconscious state. But it doesn't want to come to an end of itself by surrendering to unconditional love.

So the ego then must resort to fighting off evil impulses, and temptations to achieve the goal of being good. Unaware of the divine union of love, it's, however, incapable of being good. So the religious ego then often hides behind its well-rehearsed chapters and verses that shift the focus away from love onto the sins of others. Consider all the preachers you have heard lash out against sin in society, and then get caught in their own hypocrisy. Often their intense rhetoric against the vileness of sin is rooted in their own inner self-hatred for not being enough the way they are.

So the real story that we learned from Jesus is that reforming the ego is pointless. Obeying the Commandments was a device created by the ego that keeps us trapped in the fearful thoughts of guilt, thereby further alienating us from divine love. The writers of the Bible in the end, declare that Jesus is the end of the law, because our *I* (or the ego) was crucified with Christ, and a new guiltless person—Christ—was all of our identity.

To give you a personal example about the ego, religion, and sin, I go back into my early 20s—a period in my life that seems almost absurd today. Yet it was my reality back then, and sadly enough the reality of many sincere seekers of God. I was deeply committed to the religious system I was part of at the time. I was very sensitive to any evidence of sin in my life and was therefore afraid of what I now refer to as the god of the tree of knowledge of good and evil. I remember a prominent religious leader telling me about the evils of TV. When he walked into a hotel room by himself, he would unplug the TV and cover it with a towel. Looking back, I can see that my ego wanted to attain the same spiritual level as him. I wanted to be "anointed" like him, and have a large ministry, and would, therefore, need to pay the price by resisting the evils of TV.

Needless to say, the harder *I*—the ego—tried to resist the TV, the more I found myself being pulled in by the TV. I became fixated, and eventually, I lost to the TV, setting off another round of guilt. That guilt kept my mind in the past, while simultaneously projecting punishment into my future. While focusing on my failures, my subconscious concluded that I could never have success within my religion. God was angry with me because I could not resist the temptation of TV. I was just not good enough.

Since guilt cannot coexist with unconditional love, the guilt pushed me further away from awareness of the eternal love-union that is the ultimate truth. I was spiritually a failure and for days and sometimes weeks, I would slip further and further into a spiral of self-hatred, manifesting as unhappiness and even depression.

The guilt didn't just impact the feelings I had about myself, but it strengthened the ego's need to compare me to others. "If I can find others worse than me," I subconsciously thought, "then my own guilt can be alleviated."

Which explains why religious folks are at times judgmental of others. The ego needs to condemn others to relieve its own insecurity and guilty conscience. When we are unaware of love, we attack others, especially other groups of people—whether people of different religions, political parties, races, nations, or sexual orientations.

Ironic, isn't it? Religious people, who profess to seek God, are often the furthest away from God, because their internal operating system is based on the dualistic fallacy of good versus evil. In one of the last books of the Bible, John alludes to this irony when he says, "Everyone who loves has been born of God and knows God. Whoever does not love does not know God because God is love."[1] Talking about God, but not unconditionally loving people, was nothing more than cheap platitude.

The End of Guilt

So how can we journey back to innocence where guilt has ended? In the next section of the book, we will explore the path back home to love that ends all guilt. But here are a few thoughts to summarize what we considered in this chapter.

First of all...
You are not your mistakes!

Your failures don't define your *true self*. What happened in the past is non-existent. So the only way your history lives on is through a story of guilt you tell yourself, or through the debilitating emotion that the trauma embedded into your cellular memories. The ego may seek to convince you that your failures represent your identity. It naturally urges you to turn your mistakes into a personal label that you now must live out for the rest of your life. But that's another fallacy created by the ego. You are not your mistakes, because you are love. The more you awaken to love as your *true self*, the more the negative and toxic emotions in your cellular memories will become disempowered and deactivated.

Secondly...
Make your mistakes into a story of redemption, not guilt.

Failure is inevitable. We all make mistakes, and sometimes the mistakes are grave. But rather than telling yourself a story of guilt, exchange it for a story of redemption—how love transformed your life and turned a minus into a plus. Remember that every cloud has a silver lining. What appears to be a failure is often only an opportunity for love to bring wholeness.

Thirdly...
Quickly return to love when guilt seeks entrance into your thoughts.

Through daily loving-kindness mindfulness that we will discuss later in the book, your mind is renewed, guilt comes to an end, and new instincts of peace, grace, and love emerge naturally and effortlessly from within.

Richard Rohr, a Franciscan priest, puts it this way:

> "You accept being accepted—for no reason and by no criteria whatsoever! To put it another way, what I let God see and accept in me also becomes what I can see and accept in myself. And even more, it becomes that whereby I see everything else. This is the glue that binds the universe of persons together. Such utterly free and gratuitous love is the only love that validates,

transforms, and changes us at the deepest levels of consciousness. It is what we all desire and what we were created for. Once we allow it for ourselves, we will almost naturally become a conduit of the same for others. In fact, nothing else will attract us any more or even make much sense."[2]

PART III

THE AWAKENING

Spiritual Awakening is awakening from the dream of thought.

— Eckhart Tolle

8
THE WONDER OF WHO YOU ARE

Have you ever...

gazed at hundreds of stars lighting up the sky on a clear night,
stood on a sandy beach on an island looking out at clear turquoise water,
experienced the warmth of the sun after a chilly night,
looked deeply into the eyes of your lover,
held your newborn baby in your arms for the first time,

...and then been overcome with wonder and gratitude for the beauty of life?

Moments of awe and amazement at the human experience can be stimulating and exhilarating. When we shift consciousness from preoccupation with our thoughts to simply observing the universe and its creation, we are astonished at the beauty of life, and mysteriously feel connected to the world. In moments like these, it's not uncommon to ask, "Who am I to be able to enjoy and participate in the beauty and vastness of it all?"

These questions about the universe and our place in it have mystified philosophers, scientists, theologians, and seekers of truth for thousands of years. Throughout this book, I have, therefore, sought to guide you to an understanding of your *true self* as love. As we now embark on the third part of the book, we will delve deeper into who you are, and specifically how you can wake up to a reality that improves your life and makes the world better for everyone. We will look at spirit, faith, Christ, heart, and meditation with a new set of eyes. We will reflect on ancient mystical traditions and consider the world of quantum physics.

When I decided that I wanted to know the truth that makes me free, I had to be honest with what my faith had brought me so far. I didn't like what I saw, so I became a desperate pursuer of truth. After my healing experience of cluster headaches in January 2006, I began searching for answers that eventually led me to practice loving-kindness meditation every day. I discovered a precious treasure of love, grace, peace, and joy within me, that was beyond anything my mind could conceive. It was a pure awareness of the stillness of the *spirit* within. Out of that grew a new understanding of many spiritual texts. It was as though I had been spiritually blind, but now the veil was removed. With new perception, I found the ancient spiritual books to be fascinating texts that should be explored through the eyes of mystics.

I want to present what I discovered in this section of the book. It's reflective of my journey of transformation. Yet it would be egoic to suggest that my path toward transformation is the only path to enlightenment, salvation, or transformation. I cannot speak for other paths because they're not part of my experience. So what I share is what changed my life. I make no judgments about other spiritual experiences.

I will use metaphors, spiritual texts, and stories that I'm familiar with from my Christian background. If you come from a different tradition, please know that I'm not writing to convert you. My intention is instead to provide a broader framework by which you can explore on your own. If you've reached this point in the book, I'm confident you are already well on your way to finding your *true self* and living your best life. So I hope that you will be able to glean insights that will be helpful to your journey, because we are all in it together.

In this chapter, we will first revisit the question of who we are. To get there, we will more deeply explore the universe, God, quantum physics, you, and how it all connects. Without looking at the *whole*—the universe and the transcending force that undergirds it—how can we understand who we are? If the starting point for exploring the question of "Who am I?" begins with *me*, we will inevitably end up in the shackles of the ego. Obsessed with the conceptualized self—its survival, significance, and value—we will find very little meaning or purpose for existence. So we need to consider who we are from the widest lens possible, and then seek out a larger trajectory that brings us to where we are and where we are heading. We begin, therefore, with the vastness of the universe.

The Universe

Think about one grain of sand on the beach, then consider how many grains of sand exist on that beach. Next, imagine all the grains of sand on all the beaches in your country and your entire continent, plus all the beaches on all the continents combined. Then add all the grains of sand from all the deserts in the world (which, by the way, make up 29 percent of the total landmass of the Earth).

When you add up all those grains of sand, there are roughly (very roughly here) seven quintillion, five hundred quadrillion grains of sand on Earth. That's a lot of sand, right?

That number pales in comparison to the number of stars in the universe: there are at least 10 times as many stars as there are grains of sand on the Earth.

If you add all those stars, planets, trees, water, cats, dogs, yourself and everything else that science considers ordinary or visible matter, you will discover that it adds up to about 4.9% of the total universe. It turns out that the rest is composed of about 27% dark or invisible matter and 68% dark energy. Scientists have virtually no idea what they are. Yet we know that dark matter and dark energy contain creative intelligence that expands the universe at a blistering speed, simultaneously holding everything together mysteriously.

When you think about the brilliance, the complexity, the vastness, and the interconnectivity of the universe, it's hard to reduce it into a merely mechanical universe that you and I inhabit as essentially nothing more than robots, created by pure chance.

Many in the scientific world are also coming to the same conclusion. The probability of a creative universe without some form of principal consciousness is virtually zilch. Dr. Robert Lanza, who is considered one of the top three leading physicists in the world and was included among the Time Magazine's 100 most influential people in the world, raised the issue in his book, *Biocentrism*:

"Has anyone offered any credible suggestion for how, some 14 billion years ago, we suddenly got a hundred trillion times more than a trillion trillion trillion tons of matter from—zilch? Has anyone explained how dumb carbon, hydrogen, and oxygen molecules could have, by combining accidentally, become sentient—aware!—and then utilized this sentience to acquire a taste for hot dogs and the blues?"[1]

The universe is indeed a mystery, and our unique place in it would be weirdly bizarre and inexplicable without some transcending force underlying the whole thing. All of this brings us back to...

God

Jeffrey Kluger, an author and senior writer at Time Magazine, invokes God in an article, when he states that science is "grappling with something bigger than mere physics, something that defies the mathematical and brushes up...against the spiritual."[2]

Talking about God, however, can be like walking among landmines. I have made reference to God throughout the book using different words because we all seem to enter a discussion with certain religious and cultural perceptions, biases, and preconceptions. In an attempt to be inclusive and rethink the whole concept of God, I have therefore used various words to describe this indescribable essence: Spirit, Divine, Infinite, Transcending Reality, Ground of Being, Being, Supreme Being, Father, Creator, One, Love, Life, Light, and a whole host of other words. Not to confuse, but to simply suggest that it's impossible to reduce what is indescribable into one word. Needless to say, many of the words used to describe God have a deeper meaning.

One such name of God is the Father. Jesus often spoke of God as Father. The word was not meant to describe a man with two legs, nor was it meant to be a slight against mothers. But the word *father* in Hebrew consisted of two letters (alef and bet), which interestingly enough were the first two letters in the Hebrew alphabet. In other words, the word *father* suggested the beginning of all. The letters of the Hebrew language were originally written as symbolic images. So, for example, the two letters that formed the word *father* contained two images. The first one looked like an ox and symbolized strength because the ox pulled the plow so seeds could be sown in the ground. The second letter (bet) was pictured as an open house where the ox found its domain. So using the word Father to describe God directly conveyed that God is the foundational strength that permeates the universe. As we have learned, Paul confirms this omnipresent view of God when he writes that the Father is one, and is over all, through all, and in all.

Another intriguing concept of God is *spirit*. In ancient traditions such as Taoism and Hinduism, as well as in Greek and Hebrew etymology, *spirit* means *wind* or *breath*. You cannot see the wind or the breath, but you can feel it, experience it, and observe the effects of it. In the same manner, the word *spirit* conveyed the invisible yet supreme power of the universe. The *spirit* (closely related to consciousness) possessed with the power of knowing, acting and creating, was the vital principle of the universe. It was also the essence by which our body is animated. As we delved into in chapter 3, without the *spirit* occupying it, the body is merely a lifeless form. The *spirit* gives the body life and awareness of its own existence. Similarly, the universe without *spirit* is just a lifeless mechanical form. The *spirit* is the divine consciousness that gives the universe life.

Earlier we described God as love, and how love is the unifying essence and the highest form of energy that permeates and holds the universe together. Equivalent to one, love is the life-giving force that undergirds all matter. So when singer Justin Bieber, driver Lewis Hamilton, John in the Bible, and writers from other religious traditions make reference to God as love, then perhaps they are merely affirming an intuitive perception that love is the deepest and most meaningful force of the universe. Yet you cannot really quantify love, except you know when you are aware of it. God is love, and love is the energy that calls all matter into existence.

When we consider these prevailing thoughts about God, we recognize the common thread: God is the originator of all, the invisible Ground of Being, whose essence is Love; the Source that turns formless into form and the *divine consciousness* that breathes life into form.

YOU

But who are you? At first glance, you are a body—pretty gory on the inside, but beautiful on the outside. Science tells us all kinds of exciting things about your body. First off, it contains about 60 percent water, unless you are really lean and fit, in which case you may only contain 50 percent water. Most of the water in your body is contained inside your cells and is essential for your cells to live. While on the topic of cells, your body consists of about 75 trillion cells, give or take a few based on your size. Each cell contains hundreds of thousands of molecules with 6 feet of DNA in every cell containing 3 billion codes. It would require 1,000 books, each about 600 pages long, to write the codes for one of your 75 trillion cells.

If you examine one of your cells closely, you will discover that each cell contains about 100 trillion atoms, which means that atoms are incredibly small. What's even more surprising is that these atoms are weirdly enough 99.9 percent empty space. So if you ever feel a bit empty inside you now know why. All kidding aside, an atom is the basic unit of a chemical element that bonds together with other atoms by moving around in an endless frenetic pace of activity. This movement of energy develops into cells that combine with other cells to form a pattern, like your heart, bones, hair, and teeth, while at the same time making up your personality, habits, and memories.

By the way, atoms are not stationary. The atoms that make you who you are at this very moment may have earlier been part of Mars or Bruno Mars, Obama or Trump, an alien or your neighbor. What remains the same is the pattern, but the atoms move in and out in indeterminable directions and speeds.

And don't worry if you notice some of your hair on your pillow in the morning, because every day we all lose hundreds of strands of hair. And if you are wondering where all the dirt in your home come from, look no further than your skin, because your skin makes up 90 percent of the dust in your home. You shed about ten billion flakes of skin every day, which means that every twenty-eight days your skin is completely replaced. And every 7 to 9 years your entire body has an entirely new set of cells.

Yet YOU continue to be YOU.

Which raises the question: WHERE ARE YOU IN YOUR BODY? You are aware that you are, but where does that awareness begin and where does it come from?

First off, science doesn't have good answers to these questions. Dr. Lanza reasons that:

> "Nothing in modern physics explains how a group of molecules in your brain create consciousness...Nothing in science can explain how consciousness arose from matter...The beauty of a

sunset, the miracle of falling in love, the taste of a delicious meal—these are all mysteries to modern science."[3]

Even with the vast knowledge we have amassed, human consciousness still remains a scientific mystery.

Dr. Lanza then suggests that, "without consciousness, 'matter' dwells in an undetermined state of probability. Any universe that could have preceded consciousness only existed in a probability state."[4] He then adds that particles seem to respond to a conscious observer, interacting at some level with *life* imbedded into the universe. This is fascinating because it intimates that perception and consciousness not only shape visible reality, but that spirit and matter are more intricately connected than we initially thought. Simply put, the more we learn through the study of quantum physics, the more the line between matter and spirit is blurred.

This suggests that in spite of the constant renewing of cells in our body and the transferring of atoms between us, there is a dynamic force, a continuous presence and being—*life*—that *breathes* consciousness through us.

This leads us back to the point of this book. Your *true self* is that presence, spirit, and consciousness. You are not your ever-changing body. You are not even your thoughts, because they fluctuate, change, and evolve throughout life. Your *true self* is instead your spirit, which mysteriously has its being in your body. That spirit is not separated or divorced from God, but is one with God.

The primary purpose of your human experience is, therefore, to awaken to this truth. Initially asleep and unconscious of our real nature, we may gradually come to realize we are trapped in the mind's illusions. If not, we live out what our subconscious has been conditioned to believe. We will experience what has been coded into our cellular memories, even from past generations.

For example, interacting with impoverished children in Tanzania has allowed me to observe them, and conclude that poverty is more than just an external condition for them: it's a mindset that impacts their behavior, actions, and how they present themselves. It's a subconscious belief that guides a child even after we provide for them. That's why meeting their material needs is not enough. The cellular memories of these precious children that define them as poor must be deactivated. They must awaken to their *true self*. Otherwise, poverty lives on in subtle ways even after their lives are improved.

The point here is that when you wake up to who you are, you become conscious of oneness with God. You become aware of indescribable selfless love within. You begin to experience peace and stillness. And you start to become aware of the *presence* of God in everything.

The more you dwell in the stillness of that awareness, the more you identify with spirit as your *true self*. Out of that identification with spirit, you recognize your body as the temple of the divine *spirit*, and your mind as a tool to manifest grace in the world around you.

The mind is no longer preeminent, but serves the *spirit* as a channel by which to express the wisdom, creativity, and love of the divine. Since the *spirit's* essence is love, the words you use, the actions that you take, and the creative expressions that you engage in reflect your *true self*. You will no longer be held back by subconscious beliefs rooted in feelings of *I am not enough*. You are enough in every situation, because your *true self* knows no limits.

9

THE UNFOLDING CREATION

Science was not exactly my favorite class in high school. Maybe it was the difficulty of a subject that didn't lend itself to my impatient youthful temperament, the challenge of understanding textbooks that used words beyond my comprehension level at the time, or the fervent opposition to the subject that I had inherited from my religious upbringing. Needless to say, my mind would dutifully drift off during these classes, and instead I considered my strategy for my upcoming tennis match that afternoon or envisioned how I could get a date with that cute girl in the front row. I believed science was merely something that my young mind should not be exposed to.

The desire to know the truth had already been hijacked by fear. Science, and especially evolution, represented what was considered against God. So it was easier to turn a deaf ear to whatever compelling case could be made for evolution than to lose my faith. What I failed to understand was that faith and science were not either-or propositions. They are merely different lenses by which to look at reality. Faith is mystical, spiritual, and considers the deeper meaning of life. Science studies how the world works through observation and experimentation.

So later in life, when I began to search for truth that would set me free, it didn't take long before I became more interested in science. If I could trust science's inventions to get me on a gigantic Boeing 777 for a 15-hour flight across the ocean, and fork over a considerable amount of money for the latest Apple device, I could not turn a deaf ear to other aspects of science that were not as friendly to my religious traditions.

Of all scientific studies, evolution appeared to me as most hostile toward God. But the more I learned about evolution (and my misconceptions thereof), and the intriguing world of quantum physics, the more my eyes were opened to a beautiful reality that only strengthened my spirituality. My newfound understanding of evolution and Christ were not opposing ideas but instead pointed in the same direction. Evolution was actually the *spirit*-in-action moving us toward a new creation—the formation of Christ-centric consciousness in all humanity.

Tielhard de Chardin, the French philosopher and Jesuit Priest, proposed a similar view when he suggested that God inserted himself into the evolutionary process. De Chardin famously concluded that God unified the universe...

> "by partially immersing himself in things, by becoming 'element', and then, from this point of vantage in the heart of matter, assuming the control and leadership of what we now call evolution. Christ...put himself in the position (maintained ever since) to subdue under himself, to purify, to direct and superanimate the general ascent of consciousness into which he inserted himself."[1]

Needless to say, mentioning the word Christ in the same breath as evolution is not without challenges. If you visit an evangelical church in the United States and get the chance to speak with the pastor, ask him whether Christ and evolution go hand in hand. In most cases, he would emphatically state that the two are incompatible. Evolution contradicts a so-called literalistic interpretation of the Bible, and therefore Christ and evolution negate each other.

So when I began to find hints of an evolutionary process in the Bible, or what I now call the *unfolding creation*, I was in awe of the possibility of merging two opposing ideas. Yet I knew that some corners of religion would not share my enthusiasm. The fundamentalist's interpretation of the Bible, even though such a view contains many contradictions, denies evolution and considers it a fallacy.

Yet Christ and evolution were, in fact, similar concepts viewed through different lenses. Science dealt with the biology and physics of an evolving universe, while Christ presented the meaning behind it, and the ultimate destiny for humanity and the universe.

So in this chapter, I want to consider evolution from both a scientific and spiritual view and present support for a link between evolution and Christ. I will not cover the subject in depth, but hopefully enough to guide you in your own spiritual journey of awakening to your *true self*.

Evolution: The Spirit-in-Action

Science tells us that the universe began about 13.7 billion years ago with an event that has been coined the Big Bang. Interestingly enough, some scientific theories now suggest that before, or perhaps concurrently to the Big Bang, a mirror-image of the universe (or an anti-universe) was birthed that runs backward in time and is made of antimatter instead of matter. Think of it as the Benjamin Button universe, where what happens here happens there but working backward. I know it's weird, but tell me what's *not* wonderfully strange, mysterious, and bizarre about this whole experience we call life.

The general belief among scientists is that three minutes into the Big Bang, which began as a point of singularity, particles bonded with other particles and formed into atoms. Then a few hundreds of thousands of years later, these atoms combined with other atoms and formed into molecules.

Moving ahead about 9 billion years, our solar system was formed. About 1 billion years later (or as my daughter, Sarah, calls it in *a blink of an eye*), molecules merged with other molecules to form cells. Reaching around the 13 billion mark, these cells united with other cells, which eventually shaped into systems that then developed into animals and humans.

What's fascinating about our evolving universe is that newer, and even more complex forms of life emerge whenever previously existing entities unite. The universe is seemingly relational in its fabric. As entities combine, the universe becomes a self-transcending reality that keeps moving beyond itself in complexity, depth, and unity.

By the time humans finally enter the scene, they have the extraordinary ability of self-awareness. They can observe, reflect, wonder, ponder, and analyze their own existence, and consider the meaning and purpose of life. As we have come to see, this is human consciousness.

So discussing evolution here to find our *true self* is then merely about an evolutionary movement toward more complex life forms with more significant and deeper consciousness. Therefore, perhaps a better term for evolution is *spirit*-in-action. Inherent in all things is an attraction toward what lies ahead—a deeper knowledge and awareness of the whole.

In essence, the universe is going through a process of self-transcendence with an ever-increasing awareness of the singleness of Being. Divine love is at the heart of this unfolding; it's the birthing of new creations that urges cosmic life toward greater unity in love, and more fully expresses the *spirit's* essence of unifying love through form.

So when talking about evolution, we are merely affirming that progress is the *spirit*-in-action, working through us to develop in full maturity. We are evolving biologically because we deepen in consciousness. Perhaps the next step in our evolutionary process is the kind of Christ-centric consciousness that Jesus demonstrated. Being one with the Father is also being one with the naked, the thirsty, the prisoner, the foreigner, and the sick. Being conscious is not just being aware of self, but experiencing, feeling, and participating in the Whole. It's seeing and perceiving life, not through the lens of the egoic, selfish, self-absorbed lens of what Christians refer to as the first Adam, but through the inclusive, self-emptying, egoless, non-dual, unifying, and love-pervading lens of the second Adam.

Love that removes barriers, divisions, and separations is at the heart of this consciousness. It's God revealing, unfolding, and emerging in and through us.

This leads us to the concept of Christ in the Bible because Christ is more than just a singular person in history. Christ is the unfolding of the divine in visible matter, or what some would call the next step in our evolutionary process toward greater complexity, depth, and unity.

Who Is Christ?

If you were to ask people on the street who Christ is, the consensus answer would be Jesus. Some would probably think of Christ as the last name of Jesus. Others would conclude that it's a title that Jesus was given. Although Christ was not the last name of Jesus, the word *Christ* is unquestionably linked to Jesus since Jesus was described as the Christ.

But where does the concept of Christ come from? Why was Jesus considered the Christ? What does Christ have to do with evolution? And finally, what does Christ have to do with our own transformation? So let's dig a bit deeper into the concept of Christ.

The word Christ came from the Greek word *Kristos*, but originated from the concept of Messiah in Judaism. The Hebrew word for Christ is *Masiah* or *Mashiah*, which translated into English as Messiah. The word Christ means "anointed one" and derives its understanding from Hebrew traditions where Kings and High Priests would be anointed by oil and set apart for their service to Israel. According to Judaism, the Messiah was a human leader, appointed as King, who would usher in a time of global peace on the earth.

When the Messiah would come, the Midrash Torah prophesied that there would be no more war, conflict, or hunger on earth, but everyone would be occupied with knowing or being aware of God. The consciousness of the planet would radically shift so much that even wildlife would be affected. According to the Hebrew prophet Isaiah, the wolf and the lamb, and the leopard and the goat would lie down together. Even the eating habits of lions would change to that of the ox, where they would now feast on straw rather than meat (imagine that: lions on a vegan diet). The change would be so radical that the entire earth would be filled with an awareness of God.

The general thought, however, was that the messianic rule would not come without conflict. Military force would be required to overcome the hostile powers of the world. The egoic mind sees the world through a duality of opposites. There are good people, and there are evil people. There's darkness, and there's light. Overcoming evil would occur when good people fought, killed, and annihilated those they considered evil. Ironically, when we seek to root out evil by using the tools of evil, such as killing another person even if it's done in the name of good, we become what we hate. We become evil to someone else.

It's in that context that Jesus appears on the scene in Israel. The people were looking for a savior who would free them from the oppression of the Roman Empire and bring peace on earth. The carpenter's son from a little town in Judea called Nazareth certainly didn't fit the bill as the dominant political figure they expected. Jesus spoke about God in parental terminology and introduced a new vision of God as the selfless or ego-emptying love that unites and makes all things whole.

Jesus also exhibited love and compassion for those who were considered "the least." He hung out with sinners, such as tax collectors, prostitutes, people of opposing religions, and even the soldiers of the occupying military force. Whoever came to Jesus was accepted and loved without restraint or condition. Strangely enough, Jesus was harshest on the religious elite who demanded complete obedience to the Biblical law. Exposing their hypocrisy and revealing their self-righteousness, Jesus questioned them. But not to satisfy some egoic need to be right. Instead, Jesus debated Scriptures to help them see the futility of the ego so that they would embrace love as a better way. As long as the religious elite considered themselves morally superior, the ego would maintain its collective hold—not only on them, but also on the society as a whole. But by exposing the hypocrisy of the religious system, Jesus stripped away the egoic patterns of the religious world so that even the staunchly religious would open their hearts to grace.

Even when Jesus was at his lowest point on the cross, he offered forgiveness and understanding to the ones who had betrayed him and made false accusations against him. Suffering the humiliation and excruciating pain of crucifixion, Jesus prayed, *Forgive them, for they know not what they are doing.* Jesus acknowledged that they were unconscious of the *true self*, and acted contrary to what was deeply imbedded in them.

Not only did Jesus demonstrate an extraordinary capacity for love and compassion, but he also identified with the people that others rejected. He was compassionate toward the homeless, the illegal immigrants, the criminals who were incarcerated, and the physically and mentally ill. No one escaped the bond and connection that Jesus shared. As much as Jesus was in the Father, he was in the other. His sense of self was not limited to his own human body, but his consciousness extended to the whole.

After Jesus' death and subsequent resurrection, a new view emerged among the followers of Jesus that he, in fact, was the Messiah, or the Christ. The kingdom of the Christ was not external, but residing in the hearts of humanity. The foundation of that kingdom was the egoless love that Jesus manifested.

In his writing, Paul concludes that Christ was in actuality the full manifestation of God in a physical body, also known as the incarnation. He wrote, "Christ is the visible image of the invisible God," and then adds, "that in Christ lives all the vastness of God in a human body." Christ was the embodiment of deity - God and human as one. What does the invisible and all-encompassing *spirit* look like when it shows up in humanity without restraint? Exactly like Jesus. And that's why Jesus was the Christ.

As we have seen, Paul didn't stop there in his writings. Christ was not only a title reserved for Jesus, it was the secret mystery within all creation. People in previous generations and in different times had searched for Christ without success. But the eternal treasure was never far away. It was always right there hidden underneath the rubble of the devastation caused by the egoic mind. That mind could not relate to oneness with God. The guilt that the mind produced would not accept unconditional and selfless love. The shame it felt prevented it from seeing the essence of the *spirit* interwoven with physical form. But the *spirit* was always there, waiting within for the awakening that would lead to the manifestation of the new creation: the Christ in me.

Paul then comes to an incredible conclusion. When the eyes of our heart (more about what that means later) are enlightened, then our perception will change. We shed the old self and transform into a new person with thoughts and knowledge that reflect the divine *presence* within. This new self is Christ. It's a new consciousness—not based on the duality of us versus them, good versus evil, right versus wrong. The emergence of Christ from within would transform our awareness and perception. "Here there is no Gentile, or Jew, circumcised or uncircumcised, barbarian, Scythian, slave or free, but Christ is everything, and is in all,"[2] Paul writes. In other words, we would no longer view one another through the fallacy of the dualistic mind. "Christ is all, and is in all" would be the basis for our new non-dual consciousness.

Imagine, for a moment, a world where we no longer regard one another based on gender, race, religion, sexuality, nationality, party affiliation, education, social status, and so on. If I'm as conscious of you as I am of myself, and that consciousness is anchored in an all-encompassing love, then the very essence of God would be on full display as Christ (the visible image of the invisible God) in and through me.

The exact nature of this new creation is challenging to comprehend. But if Jesus is a representation of that next stage in the evolutionary process, then observing his life through his teachings, his interaction with people, his miracles, his death, and even his resurrection and ascension should give us an idea of where we as humans are heading.

Of course, some would suggest that the Bible cannot be trusted because it's been revised and changed to conform to the various religious power structures over 2,000 years. That may be the case. Yet reading the Gospels gives us enough revolutionary ideas and concepts about a more compelling and compassionate way of life than what we have been exposed to at any time throughout history. Jesus indeed demonstrates a new type of creation beyond the egoic living that's been the basis for humanity for millennia. I will share more in upcoming chapters of what this means for us. But for now suffice it to say that Jesus is a template for where we are heading as humanity.

Not Victims of Our Human Biology

Before we consider the actual process of transmutation or metamorphosis, let's look at what we are learning from science about how our biology continues to evolve, even in as short a timespan as our lifetime. It doesn't take much insight to conclude that our thoughts determine how well we age, how long we live, our appearance, and our health. Although genetics certainly plays a role, it's not the only determining factor. Thoughts impact our physiology, which explains why one member of a pair of identical twins can develop asthma, but the other does not. Even though they have identical genetic material, their thoughts alter their genetic expression.

Until only a few decades ago, scientists believed the brain was a static and fixed organism. Using brain-imaging technology, neuroscientists have since discovered that your brain has plasticity and is malleable, and goes through changes moment by moment based on your frame of mind. During sleep each night, new nerve cells are born that are adapted to whatever pattern of thoughts are predominant. In other words, your mind actually controls your body and affects your biological structure.

A group of 79 taxi drivers in London underwent MRI scans throughout a period of four years. The study found that the more time the cab drivers spent on the job, the more the grey matter in their brain increased and enlarged their hippocampus, the spatial memory lobe in their brain. This is a part of the brain that regulates memories and navigational pathways. The structure of their brain changed to accommodate their vast amount of navigating experience.

Other studies indicate that our imagination can impact our DNA and can turn on and off specific genes. The simplest example of how we can influence our genes is through what has been coined the placebo effect. Belief (especially as it relates to our imagination) in a cure (often in the form of a sugar pill) causes us to generate real endogenous molecules which change our blood chemistry, which can in turn suppress pain.

Other research suggests that practicing compassionate mindfulness meditation for an extended period will not only alter our emotional wellbeing for the better, but it actually reduces the size of the amygdala lobe of our brain that controls emotional faculties such as fear, stress, and anxiety. Scientists are also learning more about how our thought networks are inherited and actually change the generational pattern. The implications are enormous as these findings reveal that we can alter the genetic expressions of future generations.

What I'm suggesting here is, of course, something even more profound than mere mind over matter. Your *true self*, which manifests during a practice such as compassionate mindfulness, is the eternal *spirit* that undergirds all things. When you move beyond your mind to a place of pure awareness of the divine union that permeates the universe, you gain the mind of Christ that is conscious of its oneness with God and all of creation. The structure of your brain is then also altered, creating new neural connections and increasing grey matter.

Some of the positive effects are very clear; such as the way your body is naturally healed, improved intelligence, and the ability to have empathy for others. A 7,000-person study in Germany also concluded that belief in oneness actually improves life satisfaction.

The Dalai Lama recalls an encounter with Padre Basili, a monk, who had been isolated at a monastery in Spain for five years meditating on love. "I noticed a glow in his eyes," the Dalai Lama said, adding that it represented a depth of peace of mind.

As the Christ-centric consciousness continues to emerge in and through us, what was prophesied in ancient spiritual texts may be found to be correct. The earth will be filled with the knowledge or awareness of God, impacting the entire planet. Perhaps that's what Paul had in mind when he wrote that all of creation is eagerly awaiting the revealing of the children of God. The *spirit*-in-action is moving the universe in the direction of greater complexity and consciousness, where the invisible God is fully revealed in and through humanity.

10

THE HEART TRANSFORMATION

One of the wonders of our world is the process by which a caterpillar morphs into a butterfly. After hatching from an egg, a hungry caterpillar embarks on a constant feeding regimen to grow in size. One day the caterpillar stops its search for food, hangs upside down from a leaf or twig, and spins into a shiny chrysalis. Inside its protective casing, the caterpillar transforms its body and emerges as a beautiful butterfly.

Similarly, we are destined to experience our own metamorphosis, whereby we transform into beings that manifest the *infinite* through our thoughts and our form. But what will it take for us to become who we are? How can we experience the kind of transformation where we manifest our *true self*?

While the cognitive mind is vital for gaining knowledge and comprehension, transformation does not occur as a rational process in your mind. Transformation begins in the *non-conscious*, or as spiritual texts often referred to as the *heart*. Other words that I use throughout this book for the non-conscious are *subconscious*, *the unconscious mind, and the metacognitive mind.* Although these words contain nuanced differences, the variations are minimal. So for the purpose of this book I use these words interchangeably.

When I speak about the non-conscious, I'm referring to the processes in the mind that occur automatically below the thoughts that you are aware of. These unconscious activities in your mind are not available for introspection and intelligent analysis. But they shape your thought patterns and form your sense of self.

So to get from where we are to where we want to be individually and collectively, we need a strategy and process to renew or renovate these automatic hidden thought processes in our mind. The goal is to align our unconscious mind with our *true self* of love. When love is established in the subconscious, then the automatized instincts, feelings, and desires will emerge as thoughts of compassion, empathy, and oneness. We will move from an egocentric to a Christ-centric consciousness, where love and unity with everything is an automatized intuitive perception—in other words, our identity.

Before we look at how we can experience the transmutation or metamorphosis into beings that live as love, we will consider both the neuroscience and the spiritual wisdom relating to the unconscious, the deep mind, and the heart.

Building Relationships and the Non-conscious Mind

Whenever you meet a person for the first time, especially if you want a relationship with them, you try to learn more about who they are. You may ask them questions about their family, hobbies, job, education, background, their beliefs, passions, pursuits, and so on.

While you are gathering information about the person, you are also trying to figure them out. Who are they really at the core? Can they be trusted? Does this relationship have potential? Are they similar to me? Will they be able to relate to me? What would this relationship do for me? The answer often comes to us in how we feel. We may conclude, "I feel good about them," or "There's something off about them, but I'm not sure what it is." The chemistry may be instant, or it may be lacking. We call this our gut instinct. But what's really happening here?

On the one hand, your conscious cognitive mind asks the questions and listens to the answers. This conscious mind controls what you say, what you do, and what you see. It contains all the thoughts, memories, feelings, and hopes that you are aware of at any given moment. At times, we refer to this mind as the logical mind, because it's aware of its own thought process. This conscious mind is able to process 2,000 bits of information per second. Yet no more than 10 percent of the mind's activity happens here.

On the other hand, you have a metacognitive mind at work. While absorbing more than 400 billion bits of information per second, your non-conscious mind is responsible for up to 99 percent of all the action in your mind. The unconscious controls your entire body and makes sure that it functions. It also contains the memories that you are not consciously aware of. Since you were a child, your mind has processed all external input and interpreted its meaning through the ego's perception. These memories have been stored in your subconscious, creating the subscript of your life. This unconscious subscript manifests itself in feelings that shape your thinking, thought-building, and beliefs.

So when you engage in a conversation with another person for the first time, your non-conscious mind plays a significant role in determining what you think of the person that is sitting across from you. While the cognitive mind is busy processing what the person is saying, how they look, what they are wearing, and any other information it gathers during the conversation, the subconscious uses that information to search through its rolodex of past experiences and knowledge to determine whether it's a relationship that is worth exploring.

But not only does your meta-cognitive mind evaluate the person you are with, it also takes into consideration who you believe yourself to be. Your past experiences, including traumas, and the knowledge you have gained have been scrambled together to form a non-conscious narrative about your sense of self.

So, for example, a young woman might be looking for a guy to date. But her father or past boyfriend was verbally or physically abusive toward her. Those experiences have been lodged into her unconscious mind and shaped her perception of her worth and value. The woman may be attracted to a healer type that she unconsciously believes will fix her. Or she may be attracted to bad and abusive guys because it somehow feels right. The young woman doesn't consciously know why, but somehow the inner unconscious story about herself believes it's what she deserves, or how she will be loved.

Of course, these hidden inner narratives about who we are come in different forms, and are shaped by various factors. The ego needs to feel unique and superior, and therefore takes what we learn and experience and interprets its meaning and significance. Eventually these stories of heroism, victimization, guilt, and so on form an unconscious narrative about who we are. This guides our behaviors, actions, and beliefs, and ultimately impacts how we relate to one another.

The Heart and Ancient Wisdom

I was first introduced to these unconscious biases while studying ancient concepts.

Many texts distinguished between a person's mind, soul, body, and heart. The mind was spoken about in reference to the thoughts that we are aware of; while the heart represented the non-conscious mind.

For as he thinks in his heart, so is he,[1] Solomon wrote as one of his proverbs. A person's sense of self was not based on their conscious thoughts, but the deeper feelings that are hidden. We are what we believe, but our real beliefs are not the conscious ideas and wishes of who we want to be. Instead, beliefs are deep-rooted hidden thought-patterns that we are not even aware of ourselves.

In another proverb, Solomon suggests that everything you do flows from your heart.[2] We live within certain boundaries. The heart has set these limitations. When we venture out beyond the limits of our heart, whether good or bad, it causes great stress and discomfort. That is why we often experience physical struggles when we are given opportunities that we feel we are not good enough for. We self-destruct when we move beyond the boundaries of our heart because we are slaves to the unconscious beliefs we have about ourselves.

As alluded to in an earlier chapter, I have learned working with impoverished children that giving them food, clothes, and shelter may help them stay alive. But it will not save them from a life of poverty. When a person's unconscious self-image is entrenched in poverty, the actions and experiences align with that image. Unless poverty is uprooted in the heart, the unconscious poverty mindset will continue to bring about lifelong struggles and discomfort.

Jeremiah, another spiritual writer of old, suggests that no one can understand the heart because it's deceitful. We ourselves cannot even know why we act the way we do. The original translation of the text suggests that the heart has been trampled upon because it contains footprints. Jeremiah implies that external voices and forces have shaped our unconscious sense of self. Emotional scars from the past have affected us unwittingly. Whether others made us feel inferior, inadequate, or incompetent, what they did or said left debilitating marks on our self-worth and self-identity. Which is why humanity is weak, feeble, and even sick, according to Jeremiah.

Solomon also suggested that the heart as your unconscious self-perception is so central to your current reality that even your health is established there. "A peaceful heart leads to a healthy body."[3] Another poetic proverb suggests, "A cheerful heart is good medicine, but a broken spirit saps a person's strength."[4] Written thousands of years ago, they were onto something that science is just now discovering. When we feel good about ourselves, remain happy, and live with less stress, our immune system improves and our bodies are healthier.

How Transformation Happens...

When we pursue a change in life, we often consider what new knowledge we must gain, what old habit we must lose, and what unique traits we must learn. Change seemingly requires a conscious process that involves willpower. Reading books, taking courses, and listening to various teachers are all tools we use for self-improvement. But change is hard, which is why so many people fail to live the life they want.

Transformation, on the other hand, involves an entirely different approach. Change is not its goal, even though the outcome of transformation is a new you with infinite creative potential. But when we focus on who we want to become or what we want to do, we are unconsciously expressing dissatisfaction with what we have, and insecurity about who we are.

For example, if my goal is to be a good person, I'm essentially saying that I'm not a good person right now. The dualistic mind has made a judgment about who I am, and I'm not enough the way I am. I need to become a good person to validate my sense of self to feel better about who I am. So we set out to become "good" through what we can gain and achieve.

However, transformation is the *spirit's* remodeling of who you are in your metacognitive mind. You are secure and complete in love. Nothing is missing in your life. You don't need to become something different than what you are. Your true essence is one with God. When your unconscious mind aligns itself with your true nature of love, then the instincts, feelings, and thoughts arising from your unconscious are divinely inspired. You become more creative because you are attuned to the universal mind of God. You have a purpose beyond the superficial needs of the ego. Love—not fear—is the new filter through which you observe reality.

But how can your unconscious mind be renovated with a new reality based on your *true self*? How can we awaken in our hearts to divine love?

According to David, the shepherd who became King in Israel, meditation was the way to commune with your heart. "*Meditate within your heart...and be still,*"[2] writes David. Much of what we know about meditation is thanks largely to what we have learned from eastern religions. But what many in Western Christianity don't know is that meditation was also central in the Bible. While there are more than 20 mentions of meditation, there are also a considerable number of indirect references. Paul wrote about the eyes of the heart (also translated as the deep mind) being enlightened, implying that the imagination was involved in shining the light of love in our non-conscious mind. In another letter, he encouraged the people of Colossae to set their hearts on the invisible realm of God because it would lead to putting off the old man (the egocentric self) and putting on the new man (Christ). The outcome would be a Christ-centric perception, where everything is Christ.

Throughout the history of Christianity, we have seen meditative or contemplative practices used as a means to be transformed. For example, Friar John Main emphasized centered prayer by focusing on a word or a short phrase until the presence of God filled one's heart. Many Christian mystics—such as St. Ignatius, Guigo II, Teresa of Avila, and Thomas Merton—all emphasized contemplative practices on God's love as a way to become aware of oneness with God.

In recent years, scientists have discovered many incredible biological changes occurring in the brain when people practice meditation and centered prayer around love. Some of the changes include reduced activity in the amygdala, the organ in the brain that generates anxiety and fear, blocked access to the emotional pain of the past in the hippocampus of the brain, and increased activity in the brain stem that helps the brain connect with the rest of the body through the nervous system, thus improving your immune system. Neuroscientists have also discovered that mindfulness increases the activity in the frontal lobe of the brain, which improves your emotional wellbeing, communication skills, problem-solving ability, and creativity. In other words, the brain is not static, but will instead evolve as you practice mindfulness.

I'm also fascinated with how neuroscience has concluded that loving-kindness meditation diminishes our sense of self. The boundary between the self and the object that we are meditating upon becomes blurred. We experience a rush of overwhelming love where we feel an absolute unity with all things.

So when you meditate upon God as love, you experience oneness with that love. Your unconscious mind discovers the true essence of your spirit that is one with God, which also makes you conscious of selfless love. In that awareness you find that love is who you are, not just as an intellectual concept, but as a deep inner knowing that guides your life.

Living with such consciousness not only brings about emotional wellbeing, increased intelligence and creativity, and a boost in our immune system, but it also transforms our shared human experience. Peace on earth and good will toward all are no longer unattainable concepts and ideas, but the fruit of our shared transformation. *I am love* becomes our conscious collective identity, and that revelation in our heart is essential for a better world for everyone. This is how, like the butterfly, you emerge from your chrysalis transformed.

This may be a good time to pause for a moment and reflect on—*I AM LOVE*.

11

WHEN FAITH REVEALS WHO YOU ARE

Whenever we spend this much time exploring who we are and then turn to the *infinite* for answers, we inevitably arrive at the topic of faith. The challenge is that faith is another word that comes loaded with troubling assumptions and misconceptions.

Faith is often thought of as a belief in God. But faith can also be presented as a path to God through adhering to a doctrine, following a set of moral values, or believing in Jesus or another spiritual figure. Faith may also be associated with belonging to a religion or going to a particular church, synagogue, temple, or other religious community.

These ideas about faith seem reasonable to the intellect, but as we will explore in this chapter, faith is at its core not a mental concept. When we view faith through an intellectual lens, it quickly becomes a device by which the ego can strengthen itself. Impelled by the ego, we may feel that we have the best belief system, and belong to the true church. Tribal sentiments hijack faith and structure it as a false dichotomy: in or out, good or evil, or us versus them.

In many Christian circles, faith is also perceived as the way to get God to act on our behalf. If I need God to intervene in my life, I have to believe. Whether I desire healing, increased wealth, or better relationships, faith is a prerequisite to get what I want. If I get what I ask for, then it's a sign of my faith. Here again, faith seems to strengthen the role of the ego. When something good happens that I have prayed for, my faith—as a form of spiritual prowess—is the reason for the answer. I prayed fervently, therefore God rewarded my efforts. In other words, the ego gets in the way and makes me feel special: *"God heard MY prayers," "God knew how much I needed it," "God had mercy on ME."*

Through this egoic understanding of faith, when prayers are not answered, then there has to be a reason for it. Often blame shifts to something outside of self. Whether it's God's sovereignty, the devil's attack, the spiritual climate in my region, the sin in my nation, or the lack of faith in my church, family, or spouse, the ego finds a way to justify itself and silence the fear that *I* may not be good enough for God. Yet, at other times, some people internalize the reason for the unanswered prayer by blaming it on a lack of faith, sin, or some other failure in their own life. But even this inner dialogue ultimately ends up strengthening the ego because we see ourselves—at least unconsciously—as a victim.

These various presumptions about faith stem from a perception of duality that views God as an entity separated from us. We see God as another being that exists outside of us, and hands out rewards to some while rejecting others. God determines whether we get whatever we are seeking—salvation, healing, wealth, freedom, and so on—based on praying the right prayer, believing the correct way, or belonging to the true religion, church, or group.

Of course, such a god appears petty, finite, and unjust to a skeptic. One may even conclude that such a god is an invention of the egoic mind to feel superior to others. The deity becomes an image in our likeness that justifies people like us while judging those who are dissimilar to us. With all of humankind's discoveries about the nature and enormity of the universe, such beliefs are just too challenging for agnostics, and eventually result in a general distrust of religion.

So when talking about faith, we need to move beyond logic and the intellect. Whenever we reduce faith into a mental construct, such as a belief system or statement of beliefs, we let the ego hijack faith. We fall prey to the illusion of separation. The concept of faith can obviously be discussed and communicated with words, but it ultimately cannot be understood by the intellect, for it is a perception beyond the limitations of the mind. As many spiritual texts suggest, faith is spiritual. Faith is seeing what the egoic mind cannot perceive because at its core faith is a mystery. It is an awareness of the transcending reality manifesting as selfless love. With a new set of eyes, we are conscious of our true essence, and our union with *spirit*.

Getting God to intervene in our affairs is not a hit or miss proposition based on the ego's ability to get God to respond to *my* faith and prayers. Instead, better health, peak happiness, creative thinking, emotional wellbeing, and increased intelligence are natural outcomes—the result of being aware of divine union.

The Faith of Jesus

Jesus demonstrated this kind of faith. Of course, most of us didn't have faith presented to us this way in church because Christianity at some point became a religion built on the *I-other* consciousness: you are either for or against Jesus. Faith became an issue of mentally agreeing with the so-called "Word of God." Having the correct belief system, living the right way, and belonging to the true church were all traps that a large segment of Christianity fell into as the egoic mind seized control. The end result was further division and separation. Guilt, shame, and fear resurfaced and distorted faith.

Jesus was, however, exhibiting faith rooted in non-duality. Faith for Jesus was transcending the *I-other* consciousness and unraveling *the divine* in visible matter. The writer of the book of Hebrews devotes considerable ink to explaining faith and how this faith of Jesus is the birth of a new kind of faith. The writer begins with, "Faith is the evidence of realities not seen,"[1] and then unfolds faith as the central theme throughout Israel's history. The giants of their tradition had believed that they were good enough for God, and therefore they didn't disqualify themselves for what they achieved.

Yet the writer points out that they had missed something about faith. There was something better waiting than what these women and men of old had been able to ascertain. Then the Hebrew writer suggests that Jesus had pioneered and perfected a new faith. The author writes, "looking unto Jesus, the author, and finisher of *our* faith."[2] The old Israelites had faith, but Jesus had pioneered a new faith.

What was this new faith that originated with Jesus? The Hebrew writer poetically writes that "for the joy that was set before him endured the cross, despising the shame, and has sat down at the right hand of the throne of God."[3] I admit that at first glance this text reminds me of some sermons in church from my childhood when I decided to doze off. Ancient phraseology and expressions may have that effect on some of us. But stay with me. We are getting somewhere.

Understanding what was written 2,000 years ago in a completely different and ancient language, and set in an alien culture with no iPhones, satellite TV, and Disneyworld can be challenging, to say the least. Then we have all these traditions, beliefs, experiences, doctrines, visions, dreams, books, TV-shows, movies, plays, churches, cults, schools, ministers, skeptics, and theologians that have interpreted for us what these things mean, creating an unconscious bias that now guides how we read these texts.

So before we consider this mysterious faith of Jesus, let's go back in history and look at what led Jesus to pioneer a new kind of faith.

Born Into Religion

Although historians and scholars are not sure exactly when Jesus was born, most agree that the year of his birth was probably between 4 and 6 B.C. Biblical accounts suggest that Jesus lived in Egypt at the beginning of his life, but then at some point moved with his parents, Joseph and Mary, to Galilee, a region in northern Israel.

Historians believe that the people of Galilee were the most religious Jews in the world at the time. Although Jerusalem to the south was considered the Jewish capital, the passion and the religious commitment in Galilee surpassed the devotion and piety of other areas in Israel at the time. Galilee was the Jewish Bible-belt where strong religious communities, scripture-based education, and devotion to family, nation, and their synagogues were the hallmarks of society. The people of Galilee were considered more conservative than in other parts of the Jewish territory and were more likely to resist the growing popularity of new religious thought, such as Hellenism.

The educational process for a young boy in Galilee at the time of Jesus was called Mishnah. Around the age of 5, children began their studies in Beth Sefer (elementary school), where both boys and girls were taught by a rabbi (teacher or master) to read and write their scriptures, primarily the Torah. By the time they finished Beth Sefer around 10 years old, many of the children had memorized the entire Torah. Even the ones who were not among the gifted students were intimately familiar with every passage of Jewish scriptures. Upon completion of Beth Sefer, most of the children would stay at home. The girls would take on household duties, whereas the boys would learn the family trade.

While working in the family business, the best male students would also continue their study in what was called the Beth Midrash (secondary school). There they would study the prophets and various other spiritual texts while continuing to memorize all their sacred scriptures. They would also learn to make their own applications and interpretations of these religious texts.

At age 18, a few of the most outstanding students would leave home for lengthy periods to study with a famous rabbi. These students were called *talmidims* (disciples.) Unlike the student-teacher relationship of today, a disciple was a passionate follower of the rabbi. The *talmidim* was not only listening to the rabbi's teachings, but also emulated his lifestyle to become exactly like his honored rabbi. Eventually, by the age of 30, the disciple was commissioned by the rabbi to go out on his own and make new disciples—in other words, to pass on their master's way of life and lifestyle so that it would continue generationally.

It was in this religious, educational, and cultural environment that Jesus was raised. By the time Jesus was 30 years old, he was one of a small group who were ordained as rabbis. While traditionally the most advanced students would approach the rabbi they wanted to follow, Jesus invited the ones who were considered uneducated and unqualified as his *talmidims*. They had already given up on their religious studies and were serving full-time in the family business. This rabbi, whose fame would be unequaled in human history, turned to the fishermen, hated tax collectors, and the rebels and told them to follow him. What a reversal of religious order! Love begins with what others consider less.

It didn't take long for Jesus to stand out among the teachers who lived in Galilee. The crowd recognized that he had authority—or what they called *s'mikhah*—to make new interpretations of their sacred scriptures. These interpretations and unique teachings were also referred to as the yoke of the rabbi. The imagery here was that a yoke connects the ox and make them walk in unison under the leadership of the lead ox.

So what was Jesus' yoke? We know that Jesus referred to his yoke as easy, and his burden as light. Then we know from the Gospels that Jesus' teachings were focused on the kingdom of heaven (also referred to as the kingdom of God). However, this was not unusual because it was the topic of all rabbis at the time.

The kingdom of God was something that they were waiting for. When the Messiah appeared, he would defeat the Roman occupying force and reestablish Israel's political and religious independence. This would usher in global peace in the world. While waiting for the kingdom of heaven to be established on earth, the Jewish community was commanded to follow the word of God and be obedient to the law and scriptures. It was their duty and served as a sign that they qualified for the kingdom of God.

But Jesus spoke of the kingdom of heaven differently. It was not something to be observed with the five senses, because "The kingdom of heaven is within you." The fruit of that kingdom was not military might, external religious piety, or tribal allegiance, but inward love that externally manifested itself as love for your enemies. It was peace from within that turned into peace on earth, and inner joy that brought joy to the world.

Jesus often used stories—also known as parables—to paint a picture about the kingdom of God. These teachings were frequently shocking and appalling, especially to the religious establishment. A common thread in Jesus' teachings and interactions with people was his care for those who were considered the least among them. As we have explored throughout this book, Jesus identified with the foreigners who lived in their nation, the sinners who were the outcasts of society, the women who were marginalized by traditions, and the secular elite who were disdained by the religious-political propaganda machine.

What troubled the religious establishment the most about Jesus' kingdom teaching was how God was not an object separate from them. Jesus spoke of being one with the Father. This was not only against their teachings, but it was also blasphemous. Their minds could not comprehend union with God because they identified with their personal and collective ego. Since fear is essential to the egoic mind, they felt attacked by a message of oneness with God because it would inevitably weaken their hold on the religious and political power structure. It would upend the authority they had worked so hard to achieve. So Jesus had to be silenced.

As history teaches us, it's not uncommon for religious systems to align with political power when they feel threatened by a progressive agenda and new spiritual thought. Voices that advocate for greater equality, tolerance, and acceptance of everyone must be squashed before they diminish the significance, specialness, and superiority of a religion. Even if that means hypocritically rejecting their most valued beliefs, it's the price they are willing to pay. It's not just their religion that's coming under attack, but it's what has set them apart as being closer to God than others.

So even though the religious leaders at the time eloquently affirmed their own law, including "You shall not kill," they were so blinded by hatred for what Jesus represented that they stirred up the crowd to shout, "Crucify Jesus!" Jesus and his message were a threat to their beliefs, their way of life, and their power. They even felt justified to break their most revered law so that they could stop progress and maintain their influence on society. Religion will, ultimately, always side with what preserves its traditions, even if it means violating its core principles. So under the banner of God, Jesus was condemned to the most gruesome death.

It could be easy to feel a sense of resentment and anger looking back at the religious and political system. Except...

Jesus knew the cross was coming. Even before he made the journey to Jerusalem, he was completely aware of what he would face. Death was somehow his mission.

Interestingly enough, Jesus never became hateful or vengeful toward his attackers. Establishing fault would only bring about further division and would pit groups of people against each other. His death could end up as just another device to strengthen the ego. The dualistic mind could use what symbolized the end of the ego to pit others toward the evil side on its continuum of good and evil. Jesus, therefore, extended forgiveness and added that they didn't know what they were doing. In other words, there was no one to blame. Jesus simply accepted his death for what it was. There was an inner joy because he was aware of the transcending reality beyond his suffering. Somehow the death would demonstrate the essence of love. It would serve as a catalyst to tear down the wall of separation that existed in the minds of humanity.

The resurrection was not a new concept among the rabbis who taught about the kingdom of God. The Pharisees, the most prominent religious group in Israel at the time, believed that the resurrection of the dead would occur when the Messiah came. After all, it had been 500 years since their exile from Babylon, and many had died. So they didn't want them to have died for nothing. Resurrection from the dead was, therefore, the promise to all of them while they waited for the coming of the Messiah and the establishment of the kingdom of heaven on earth. It was a reward for all the faithful Jews.

So when the story of Jesus' resurrection was told, it was not a new idea, but it had a new twist to it. Only one Jew was raised. Later when Jesus' disciples begin to put the pieces together, it occurred to them that the forthcoming resurrection as the "world to come" was already here—or at the very least it had already begun. A new age of the Messiah had dawned. A future world was invading the present.

But the resurrection life was nothing like what they had foreseen. The resurrection of Christ was a consciousness emerging from within each and every one of them. The kingdom of heaven was a dimension within them where they were united in love with the transcending reality. Moving beyond the egoic mind and finding their *true self* in the *presence* of God was their resurrection from the dead. The end of physical life was only a transition into another form.

The Faith of Jesus Unfolds Who He Is

After the dust had settled and all the followers of Jesus looked back at what had happened, they realized that Jesus had pioneered and perfected a new faith unlike any they had seen before. The Hebrew writer poetically put words to what many had been feeling inside. The faith of Jesus was beyond what they had ever imagined.

First off...
The faith of their rabbi revealed that suffering death on the cross was not the end, but the beginning.

That faith was not based on a statement of beliefs, but on an inner joy from that dimension within Jesus that is one with the deity. Jesus endured the horrifying death of crucifixion so that they could discover the secret of life: to die before you die is simply learning that there is no death. As followers of the way of Jesus, their fate may not be the same as Jesus. But their crucifixion story was the death of the ego. Faith for them was the inner joy they felt when they experienced pain, knowing that suffering was necessary for the death of the ego. But the pain was only temporary. The resurrection—awakening, enlightenment, salvation, transformation—was the inevitable outcome.

Then secondly...
The faith of Jesus revealed that the shame that had been passed down from Adam was only an illusion.

Shame, the feeling that *I'm not enough*, had entrenched itself in their subconscious, guiding them in never-ending external pursuits for love, significance, and superiority. Always trying to prove their worth, humanity was in a continuous struggle to be good and avoid evil. Eating the fruit from the tree of knowledge of good and evil had hidden the dimension within them of pure love and joy in the *presence* of God. But Jesus had faith, as evidenced by his inward joy, and thought nothing of shame. Jesus was conscious of oneness with divine *presence*. The kingdom of God was inside him. The Garden of Eden was that dimension in him that was naked and not ashamed.

Thirdly...
The faith of Jesus revealed to him that he is the Son of God.

Now it was not uncommon at the time for people to consider themselves children of God. Yet to be the Son of God was different. The son of a king sat on the right hand of his father's throne because he was no longer a child. Possessing and demonstrating the same nature as his father, the son had authority in his father's kingdom and was, in fact, equal to him. The expression *son of god* was also common in the Roman world, where they had many gods. From Jupiter as the protector of the state, Mars as the god of war, to Isis as the goddess of fertility and the mother of death and rebirth, the gods came in many forms. These gods would at times get together for some "wine and romance," and soon a son would be born, who exhibited the same qualities as the gods. Since the primary characteristics of the deities at the time were power, wealth, war, and fame, emperors such as Julius Ceasar and Augustus were called the Sons of God.

In the case of Jesus as the SON OF GOD, the Father was the omnipresent transcending invisible Presence of Love that is above all, through all, and in all. So to be the Son of God was to dwell in a human body, and yet possess and demonstrate the Christ-consciousness rooted in selfless love and oneness with all. Everyone was a child of God, but to be the Son of God was to manifest the deity in fullness through the mind and the body. For the early Christians, Jesus was the exact image of the invisible God: the logos that existed in the beginning and became incarnate. If you wanted to know the true essence of the mysterious and the all-encompassing Source of Life, you only had to look to Jesus. He was the Son of God who defined what God is in a human body.

What made the story of Jesus so fascinating for much of the known world at the time was that divine sonship was not just reserved for the rich and powerful. But Jesus had provided a path for all of humanity to unravel the divine Son in them. Jesus' mission was to attach his yoke around them to guide them. As they would look at Jesus, his faith would be their faith—not as a doctrine, but as an inner awareness of oneness with the Father whose essence is Love.

Is the Faith of Jesus Relevant to Us?

We began this chapter by suggesting that faith reveals who we are. After learning about the faith of Jesus, we are left to ask ourselves whether Jesus' faith is vital to us today. Two thousand years have passed since this fascinating, mystical, and divine figure named Jesus spent 30-some years in a small corner of our globe. Yet the story of Jesus has lived on and become one of the most celebrated stories in human history. Some suggest that the story has seen its best days. Church attendance is declining, especially among the younger generations. Technology and the ability to travel will eventually make us less suspicious of each other. We will become more open to exploring different spiritual and religious streams.

So when we look at Christianity as a religion, we may have doubts that it can survive another century or two, let alone millennia. It's not because we may not find Jesus significant—quite the opposite is often the case. But it would seem to me that if Jesus is presented as an *either or, good versus evil, in or out* proposition, then the Messiah will remain little more than a weapon of the ego that desperately wants certainty, validation, and to be proven right. When the "Jesus-gun" is pointed at us, and we're told, "Either you believe and follow Jesus, or you are going to Hell," then this Jesus story just doesn't sit well with what we intuitively perceive as the divine among us.

Imagine a world leader calling for unity in the world. But there's a catch: in order to earn this unity, everyone would need to swear allegiance to him, and follow him even if they know what he says is false. Many would obey him out of fear because, after all, he has the most power in the world. Others would be attracted to him because they see him as the authority figure they never had. To some, he would be similar to their own father, whose approval they always sought. In the end, most of the world would either openly or secretly reject the leader. It certainly would not lead to unification, at least not a unity of the heart based on love.

Similarly, the story of Jesus cannot be the answer to the world if it's presented as the true religion. Such proclamations will always carry the stench of the ego's need for control. But what if Jesus is not a religious founder, nor a device by Christianity to decide who is in and who is out?

What if Jesus is instead a face to behold, arms to embrace, and feet to follow in finding divine love within us?

The egoic consciousness has warped our minds. We are terrified. Anger, abuse, addiction, obsession, depression, selfishness, greed, corruption, and violence are symptoms of our inner hell. Fear is our shared lovelessness. The blindness of our collective hearts is the cause of the divisions between us. When we look around and see inequality, intolerance, unrest, hatred, racism, xenophobia, homophobia, violence, murder, mass shootings, and war, we cannot help but wonder whether there is a better way.

One ancient writer suggests that all of "creation eagerly waits for the revealing of the sons of God." But to get there, the voice of the ego must die, so that we can learn how to live. It's here that the faith of Jesus can serve humanity today. When religious baggage that has been piled on the rabbi from Galilee is incinerated, then Jesus can be more relevant than ever.

Pure, unselfish, and unconditional love will be more than abstract ideas and vague concepts. Love will be remarkably human. Following the light that was Jesus can then guide us in unraveling love as our true essence. In that awareness of oneness with *spirit*, the Christ-centric consciousness can emerge and make the world better for everyone.

12

HOW MEDITATION HELPS YOU AWAKEN

My first introduction to meditation was in early 2006. I have often wondered why out of nowhere I felt an urge to meditate when I was experiencing excruciating pain. The concept of meditation was utterly foreign to me and, quite frankly, frightened me.

Yet, as I walked down a set of stairs, wholly overwhelmed with these recurring cluster headaches, I suddenly knew that I had to meditate on the profundity of the love demonstrated by Jesus. Within a couple of minutes of slumping into the seat of a black Nissan Maxima and closing my eyes, I was overcome with a feeling of love. When the pain then disappeared, it was a moment like no other for me. The despair and helpless feeling that had weighed me down suddenly disappeared.

Of course, since that moment, my understanding of meditation has evolved. Loving-kindness mindfulness and contemplation is now a daily practice for me. When I first began to practice mindfulness consistently, I observed that I was less anxious, worried, and stressed. My blood pressure also drastically improved, and I felt better overall than I had for a long time. I also noticed that feelings of guilt and fear subsided, and many of my insecurities faded away.

Then in 2012, I put together a 40-day meditation challenge called Amazing Life. Before it was officially published, a friend in the Netherlands asked if I would send it to him to preview. At first, I was not eager to share the program because I was concerned about whether it would be accepted. But I emailed him the audio files anyway. About 3 weeks later, he excitedly called me and told me of its impact on his life. Within a short period, he had personally involved hundreds of people in the program on several continents. Since then we have also translated the Amazing Life mindfulness program into Dutch, Spanish, and Swahili. It's now being used in Africa, Europe, Asia, South America, and here in North America as a resource to help people experience oneness with divine love.

The reports I have received from people whose lives have been dramatically impacted by these meditation exercises are beyond anything I could have ever imagined. Whether it was Lois, the woman raised as an orphan, who used the meditations to help her overcome decades of nightly occurrences of nightmares, or Richard from California, who used them to cure many years of insomnia, these simple daily exercises work for so many because the meditations are designed to heighten awareness of transcending love.

One amazing testimony involves a young mother, Debbie, who after being diagnosed with terminal brain cancer, began practicing the Amazing Life meditations. At first, Debbie was skeptical. But as she persisted, she found herself overwhelmed with the purity and power of love. Six months later, while going through a routine scan of her brain, they discovered that her tumor had dissolved. All the symptoms of cancer had also disappeared. The doctor subsequently gave Debbie a clean bill of health.

What Is Meditation?

Before we get into the specifics of the meditation introduced here, let's briefly look at what meditation is.

The word *meditation* merely means heightened awareness, or contemplation, and implies being present in the now. In other words, in meditation the mind is not obsessively focused on past experiences, or future events, but is instead one with the moment. There are numerous benefits to any secular or spiritual mindfulness practice that disengages us from the trappings of the egoic mind.

What I'm presenting here, however, is a meditation that heightens awareness of divine love. Mindfulness is not the goal itself, but merely a path to experience oneness with the Source of Life. Since the mind has made us unaware of the divine life that lies within all of us, meditation is a practice that leads to a place of awareness of God.

This brings us to Calvin Cordozar Broadus Jr., also known as Snoop Dogg. Yes, the famous rapper, singer, and American pop culture personality. The story of Snoop Dogg begins in Amsterdam. I was about to fly from Amsterdam to Los Angeles on a Boeing 747. With seats reserved in the upper deck business class, I was hoping for a restful and relaxing flight. When I checked in at the counter, I was informed that the airline had to move me a couple rows back because there was a group traveling together. The upper deck on this Boeing 747 only had 18 seats, so it didn't make much of a difference to me.

Yet it was an unusual request, so when the flight finally took off for its 11-hour trek from Amsterdam to LAX, I looked over at the area where my original seat was. I noticed three African-American gentlemen who seemed to be traveling together. Two of them were big muscular men who looked like they could be NFL linebackers. Beside them was a lanky gentleman. Since I didn't recognize any of them, I didn't think much more about it and settled in for the long journey.

At one point on the flight, I noticed the flight attendants whispered to each other, and one of them asked the lanky gentleman to sign something.

When we were about 20 minutes away from landing at LAX, it suddenly dawned on me that the gentleman was Snoop Dogg. So I asked the flight attendant, and she confirmed my hunch. I had spent almost 11 hours in the presence of Snoop Dogg, but I wasn't aware of it and therefore being on the same flight with him had no consequence on me, positive or negative.

Besides a good story to tell my kids, being in the presence of Snoop Dogg doesn't make much of a difference to me personally. (Hearing the life-story of Calvin Cordozar Broadus Jr. would have been far more impactful.) But there's a point here that illustrates the goal of meditation.

We are always in the *presence* of the divine *spirit*. In fact, God lies within all things while still transcending them. So in the same way that I was in the presence of Snoop Dogg for 11 hours without knowing it, we are not aware of our union with God.

Sitting on a flight with Snoop Dogg didn't benefit me because I was unaware of his presence. I didn't ask for a selfie or an autograph for my children. I never discussed my books or my ideas with Snoop Dogg. I never learned the inside story about being a rapper. And yes, I likely wouldn't have approached him even if I were aware that he was on the flight. But the point is that being in the presence of someone or something doesn't make a difference to us unless we are aware.

This illustrates the goal of mindfulness. Meditation is a pathway to move from self-awareness to spirit-awareness, where you are conscious of oneness with God. As you meditate daily, you will gradually experience an increasing awareness of divine love where you feel a sense of unity with all things. You awaken to your *true self* as an embodiment on earth for the limitless divine life.

The Garden Within

When I was a child, I was intrigued by where the Garden of Eden might be located. I'd consider the likely locations based on scholarly theories, and would even search out maps to see if I could find this mysterious place. I would even dream of traveling to such places as Iraq where the Tigris and Euphrates rivers run into the sea, the supposed location of the Garden of Eden.

But similar to the book *The Alchemist*, where the young Andalusian shepherd traveled the world in search of a treasure, only to finally realize it was right there where he first began, the Garden of Eden is always right here as a hidden dimension in you.

But how do you find this treasure within you? What's the path to the presence of God where you find your *true self*?

Begin With Gratitude

Consider for a moment that meditation is a mode of transportation with several stops to your favorite destination in the world. But rather than heading someplace far away, you are on a journey to the eternal place of unbridled innocence, happiness, and peace within you. You are on a trek to find your *true self* in paradise.

To get there, you begin with *gratitude*—the launching pad, entry point, and departure gate for your journey. As you embark on this trek, you first discover that the language is different. Every consciousness has a language. The various egoic stages of consciousness are essentially self-centered and speak the language of arrogance, pride, self-loathing, victimization, selfishness, dishonor, anger, and scarcity. It pits people, nations, races, religions, and groups against each other. But the Christ-centric consciousness that's infused with love speaks a different language. It is grateful because it knows that everything in life is a gift.

Gratitude is not only a verbal communication or mental response to what you are facing. At its core, being thankful is an inner experience of fullness, an expansion within you, and an opening of your heart. You shift your consciousness away from the need to establish blame, assess fault, and assign good and evil, to a place of gratefulness for all things. What you are facing cannot be denied. Yet the need to discern its worth as either good or bad will only imprison you in your fearful stories. When you instead give thanks in every situation, you let go of the ego's need to judge and open your heart to become aware of love.

So as you meditate, find a quiet, peaceful, and secluded area. Personally, I prefer outside in my backyard when the weather permits. There is something majestic and celestial about nature. But some of my most significant experiences have been indoors. Whatever the location, look around at everything and express gratitude with your heart. Let your mind wander for a few moments, but no more than 60 seconds. Convey gratefulness for what life has brought you. Even when painful memories emerge, simply observe them. Your egoic mind will try to attach itself emotionally to the past and define who you are. But you are not the sum total of your history. When you cease to identify with your thoughts and remain in a state of gratefulness, then the emotional sting will begin to fade. The more you practice, the easier it gets.

After expressing gratitude for a short period, begin your meditation. Find a chair and sit down in an upright yet comfortable position. Make sure you stay in a quiet and secluded area. Put your earplugs in and listen to soft meditation music quietly in the background (you can find guided meditation by visiting davidyoungren.com).

Then close your eyes, and take a few deep breaths. Hold your breath for several seconds before you release it slowly. As you take these deep breaths, you will become more fully present and calm. Focus on your breath while you remain in a place of gratitude. The journey to that sacred place in you where you are aware of the Presence has begun.

There will be distractions along the way. You may be tempted to break off and quit the meditation many times, and sometimes you will. That's okay. Each time you resume this mindfulness prayer, the easier it becomes. At some point, the trip will be much shorter, and eventually you will arrive at that point within you where you are aware of divine love.

Peace in Your Body

Peace is the first stop in our journey toward awareness of divine *presence*. When your body is under stress, especially for extended periods, your energy drains and your body begins to break down. You may experience headaches, muscle tension, chest pain, fatigue, sleep problems, stomach issues, and a change in sex drive.

These symptoms make it difficult to experience any deep awareness of God within you. The tightness and nervous tension in your body needs to be released. Your body has to return to a state of peace, inner rest, and a sense of harmony.

So as you begin your meditation, focus on the word *peace*—slowly and quietly repeating it inside of you. With every breath you inhale, mentally observe peace flowing through your digestive system, all the way down your body, and then back up again through your brain before settling in your heart. Make sure to focus on every part of your body to the point that you can feel every tension. When you feel a tension in a certain area, release that tension by exhaling, while simultanteously focusing on peace resting in that part of your body.

Since my background is Christian, I have found that incorporating the words of Jesus into this exercise is beneficial. I imagine Jesus standing in front of me, speaking to me tenderly: *"Peace I leave you. The same peace that I have I give to you... Don't let your heart be troubled, neither let it be afraid."* Then I briefly let my mind be reminded of Jesus' words after his resurrection, when he gently breathed on his followers and said, *"Peace be with you...Receive the Holy Spirit."* My body is the temple of the Holy Spirit. In the same way that God in the outset of Genesis breathed *spirit* into the body of Adam, Jesus breathes the divine life of peace into my body. If you are comfortable with it, you can try a similar approach by first paying attention to the words while you inhale. Then focus on the peace of the Holy Spirit flowing through your body removing and releasing all the tension and stress.

Continue this exercise until you are aware of an inner rest, calm, and peace throughout your body. This will only take a few moments when you have been meditating for a while. In the beginning, you may find it challenging. But hang in there. The more you practice the presence of peace in your body, the more quickly you will feel the effect of eased tension. Your immune system and health will gradually begin to improve as stress is reduced.

Grace for Your Heart and Mind

Next, we move to grace in your heart and mind. To find your *true self* in paradise, grace must permeate your subconscious. Grace is the antidote to the ego. The ego, which has edged God (Unconditional Love) out to live by the value system of the tree of knowledge of good and evil, gets its worth and significance by earning acceptance, approval, and love through its own efforts. Any success we achieve is justified by crediting our hard work. Whatever good happens to us, we deserve because we are self-made.

This mindset ingrained in your subconscious cannot accept unconditional love. The ego reasons that "if there is a God, and that God is going to help me, then I must do something to deserve that help." Whether believing, praying, going to my place of worship, being a good person, giving toward good causes, being loving toward family, obeying the rules of my religion, or reading my sacred texts, the ego will always find something to rationalize why God brings favor and success.

Grace is counter to every egoic instinct you have because the essence of grace is unmerited favor. In many ancient spiritual texts, the word *grace* was used to describe a process by which one comes to the end of the ego and finds a new consciousness emerging from within. The ego yields to undeserved favor.

While many of our traditions get at least a semblance of that story, grace is often presented as a mental concept rather than as a transformation from the inside out. But to the ancient writers, grace was not another religious doctrine to separate the sinner from the saint. Grace was a transformational process of the heart. As we explored earlier, the heart was an ancient description of what today is commonly referred to as the unconscious mind or the subconscious.

These early Christians viewed the death of Jesus as the tangible expression of grace. When the profundity of grace would permeate the subconscious, it would open the heart to accept God without condition. The egoic mind could never receive unconditional love because it had to perceive itself as being deserving of love. But grace, as shown in Jesus—an image that was relatable—was a way for these Christian mystics to experience freedom from the egoic patterns in their subconscious, so that they would no longer resist unconditional love, or disqualify themselves from the divine presence of love. Their terminology was slightly different from what I use, but the concept is similar.

Two millennia later, grace in most of Christendom is often portrayed as the opposite of its intent. Viewed through the dualistic mind, grace becomes a matter of right and wrong, in or out, and good versus evil. Grace is associated with tribal religion in service of the rational mind or the ego, rather than a deep mystical transformational path to awareness of unconditional love.

Accepting the spirit of grace is, however, different because it involves surrendering the need to win, to be right, to be first, to be special, or to stand out. These are the ego's never-ending pursuits that only lead to suffering. But when the subconscious permeates with grace, then it opens the door to the *spirit* (energy) of love to flow unhindered through your heart and into every cell in your body. I'm convinced that this divine grace will also empower your mind with increased intelligence. Creativity will flow more naturally as your mindset is aligned with undeserved favor.

This brings us back to mindfulness, and how to incorporate grace into your meditation. Once you have come to the point of peace within, create an image in your mind of grace flowing from the top of your head all the way through your chest, stomach, and down through feet and back up again, before finally settling in your mind. The Hebrew wisdom writer, Solomon, poetically penned that wisdom will "place on your head a garment of grace." It surrounds, protects, and creates beauty in your mind.

While focusing on grace surrounding your head, quietly repeat the word *grace*. Your life—breath, mind, and body—is undeserved favor. Everything you accomplish flows from undeserved favor. Nothing you do or say adds anything to your worth. Your intelligence, abilities, gifts, talents, and the propensity to work hard are all undeserved favor. When you are weak, you are strong because everything is merely grace. As you stay focused on grace, the ego will become less prominent in your mind. The need to prove yourself—your worth, value, and significance—will dissolve and your heart will open itself to your spirit.

Remember, you cannot deserve love, work for it, or be good enough to receive it. Nothing can separate you from divine love. You can only wake up to love as the eternal *presence* of God. Meditating on grace brings you to the place deep within where your mind will no longer reject unconditional love. From that place, your heart is wide open to God.

Finding Heaven Within You

Being conscious of God is being aware of unconditional love. When grace permeates your consciousness, then you become aware of the divine *presence*. It's in that awareness that you find your *true self*—your spirit. Your identity is not a mental concept, nor is it your body. Your thoughts and your physical appearance are always changing. But what remains is spirit or pure consciousness.

When you practice this meditation consistently, you may reach a point where you cease to identify with your body and mind. You are aware of the *presence* and conscious of selfless love. In that awareness, the line of separation between God and you are blurred. You feel oneness with God. The infinite *presence* that is beyond comprehension is somehow one with your *true self*. You will also begin to experience and feel the divine *presence* in everyone and everything. The divine mystery that "Christ is all, and is in all" will become more than a mental concept, but a profound inner revelation. As Jesus identified with "otherness," you will also see yourself in people you once defined as "other."

During this stage in your meditation, focus on the word *love*. You may even experience a voice of awe within you calling out *Father*. The word *Father* here is not so much a masculine pronoun as it is an affirmation of your relational union with the transcending reality of the universe. You have found the essence of your *true self* as a son of God (a term beyond gender). Love is the essence of your *true self*. You are a reflection of the outpouring of God in visible matter. A deep sense of love, joy, and peace wells up within you. You have found the hidden mystery—paradise and the kingdom of heaven—as a reality beyond logic and your intellect.

My experience is that these moments are not always the same in your meditations. There are some days that you may not feel much of anything. Then there are other times when you may only have brief flashes—a few seconds—of awareness of the divine *presence*. Yet I have seen so many people experience physical healing and find freedom from shame, pressure, addictions, grief, depression, and every kind of fear even during these moments.

The more often you put these meditations into practice, the more you will notice a corresponding improvement in your emotional and mental wellbeing. You will feel differently about yourself. Any guilt or feeling of *I'm not enough* will fade. Challenges and problems will no longer "hook" you emotionally as they did in the past. Feelings of anxiety, worry, stress, anger, and depression will diminish, and you'll notice a continuous peaceful hum within you that guides you throughout the day.

You will also have more empathy toward others. Even past offenses will seem less important, and you may find yourself—even if it is just briefly in the beginning—seeing reality through the eyes of the so-called offender. The egoic tendencies of judging, ranking, and putting others on the evil side of the spectrum will be replaced with compassion, forgiveness, and generosity. You'll discover that love has always been there, and you may have simply been unaware of its presence. If it takes you a long time to make this realization, that's just fine. Remember: I'm the guy who didn't even realize Snoop Dogg was on his flight.

PART IV

THE MANIFESTATION OF YOUR TRUE SELF

Our purpose here on earth: to manifest the very nature of our spirit, which is touched by the spirit of God.

— RUMI

13

A MINDSET OF LOVE

When you find your *true self* within, you gain a new view of yourself and the world. You realize your mind has been under the control of an egoic consciousness. What unfolds upon that realization is a total renovation where love—not fear—increasingly becomes the primary guide of your thoughts, feelings, and beliefs. As the mind experiences this radical shift in perception, your vision is enlarged. Limitations of the past are broken, and like an eagle, you'll effortlessly soar to new heights. The memories of the "old you" become just a distant, incoherent dream because the way you view reality now is the polar opposite from how you perceived things then.

Paul, the ancient scribe, writes mystically that the mindset of grace lifts us from an earthly fear-based perception to a heavenly view of love, where Christ is all and in all. In other words, the revelation of your *true self* within broadens your perspective.

One of my most treasured opportunities has been to start a charity called Juma's World that empowers children in Tanzania. Our main work is located in and around Tabora. In the beginning, we would travel by flight to Tabora, landing on a hilly graveled landing strip. But then all flights were canceled for several years as they rebuilt the airport. During this time, we would first fly to a city called Mwanza and then embark on a torturous eight-hour drive on some of the worst roads ever created to get to our final destination. Throughout the rainy season, the route was especially treacherous—the rain had pounded the gravel roads to create huge potholes. We had to hold onto our seats just so our heads wouldn't bang against the roof of our vehicle.

On occasion, the roads got the best of me. Oscillating between anger and self-pity, I would complain and promise myself that I would never again make that trip. Of course, memory quickly fades with time, so I journeyed that road more times than I'm willing to admit.

Until 2014...

While searching online, I found a small airline that flew passengers to different towns in that area. I contacted them, and they agreed to put me on a flight that would make a stop in Tabora just for me. And they would only charge $180. I thought I had hit the jackpot. So I made the flight from Mwanza to Tabora in about an hour. Sitting in the cockpit, I looked down and noticed the beauty of the terrain, the charm of the roads that strikingly wove themselves throughout the astonishing countryside. Up in that "heavenly" realm, my view shifted. Whereas before I had focused on the potholes on the earthly terrain, now I was enamored with my view of the stunning landscape. The aggravation and misery had turned to inward peace and gratefulness.

In the same way, finding that "kingdom of heaven" within you will transform your worldview. Exchanging fear for love as the primary lens of perception will radically change how you feel and what you believe about yourself. What used to trigger anger, anxiety, worry, loneliness, despair, and unhappiness will no longer faze you as it did in the past. You will experience calm amid confusion and an inner joy even when circumstances are not going your way.

Your view of people will also shift from negativity and judgment to hopeful and life-giving. Forgiveness toward those who have offended you, empathy for people who are different from you, and generosity to the ones who are struggling will naturally emerge. It's a path to a better and more equitable world.

Let's explore this mindset a bit further, including some of the attitudes and behavioral changes that we can expect as we grow in awareness of divine love.

The Confident Mind

Rejection is probably the most common emotional wound that we experience in our lives. When our spouse leaves us, or we get passed up on a promotion, or excluded from a social gathering, we experience the sting of rejection. The emotional pain that we feel can be absolutely paralyzing.

Our bodies may also experience physical pain. fMRI studies indicate that the area of the brain that activates physical pain is also triggered when we experience emotional rejection.

Rejection is also a cause of mental illness. According to a report by the Surgeon General of the United States, rejection increases the potential for violence in a teenager even more than drugs, poverty, and gang affiliation. School shootings and violence against women are also strongly linked to rejection.[1]

But for most people, the devastating effects of rejection are limited to emotional instability. We may become self-critical, depressed, disgusted with ourselves, and even self-destructive. Our IQ is lowered as the rejection prevents us from thinking clearly. Our body language and social behavior are also affected. We revert into a shell and may spend less time with friends and family. Even when we are forced to be around people, we struggle with eye-contact, smiling, and often look down rather than keeping our head held high.

Rejection is ultimately rooted in shame. We feel like we are not enough to be loved and accepted. There's something wrong with us, and the debilitating emotions surface as a way to punish ourselves. When the pain becomes unbearable to carry on our own, we may resort to exerting punishment on the ones who contributed to our pain. The ego wants them to suffer like we are suffering. Whether it's through a cold shoulder to the offender, or something as drastic as violence, the ego projects its own self-hatred for not being worthy enough of the other's love.

The good news is that something extraordinary and beautiful happens when you awaken to love within. Your confidence is no longer based on what people do to and for you. Love is not an external gift that you earn or deserve, but is instead the inward awareness of divine love flowing through you.

So when you are with people, you are able to extend love to them even if they reject you. You are able to offer them a smile, a hug, direct eye-contact, and complete attention. Their response to the love that you offer is immaterial because your security and confidence is an internal state of being one with divine love. What you will most often find is that the love that is emanating from your heart will attract people to you. They will inevitably be less likely to reject you. And even if they turn against you, you will not take their rejection as a personal insult. Instead, you will strangely enough experience empathy and compassion for them because you recognize in them the pain that fear has produced.

This is why being conscious of love will inevitably result in a genuinely confident mind. Your confidence will, however, not be based on the ego's sense of worth through your success (which is actually insecurity with a self-assured mask on). Instead, your confidence will derive from that deepest part of you that is one with divine love.

The Strong Mind

Since childhood, we have been taught to associate vulnerability with weakness. Letting others see our hurts, failures, and imperfections is such a daunting challenge for most people that they keep everyone at a safe distance, always giving themselves an exit strategy in every relationship. One young woman once came to me with a vulnerable confession. She said, "I have always tried so hard to be strong. I don't let anyone in because I'm afraid I will be rejected. Whenever someone gets close enough to see my vulnerabilities, I find an excuse to run away from the relationship." She had to stop before the tears overwhelmed her.

We are so afraid to appear weak because the ego has hoodwinked us into thinking that flawless perfection is the only way we will be loved and accepted. Since the nagging voice inside is quick to point out our faults and remind us that we are not enough, we hide behind impenetrable masks that show off our abilities, talents, knowledge, and wealth. No one can really know what we are like because an open heart leaves us exposed to attack and what we assume will be more pain.

But when you discover that your true essence is one with divine love, vulnerability is reframed not as a weakness, but as strength. Without vulnerability, the ego will hold your mind captive to the fear of being exposed. But the moment you let others in to see your imperfections, you give permission for love to heal and make the broken pieces whole.

One time I was coaching Aislynn, who had a dream of owning an investment property. Most of my initial sessions involve reframing a person's mindset. Fear and insecurity are usually the biggest obstacles for people to overcome. That's why in the early sessions, I guide people toward finding their *true self* within: so they will have the confidence to accomplish their goals. But working with Aislynn, I noticed that she experienced unusual resistance. Although she wanted to own property, Aislynn disqualified herself and didn't think she had what it takes. Then in one session, I encouraged her to look within to identify what was holding her back. Suddenly she broke down in tears and shared how her ex-husband had always put her down and made her feel inadequate. For the next 30 minutes, Aislynn revealed her life story. At that moment something shifted inside her. Aislynn exposed her perceived weaknesses, and that became the turning point for her. Being vulnerable had opened her to allowing love to heal her broken heart. When her heart was whole, Aislynn was able to take action on her dreams. Sharing her perceived weakness was the fuel she needed to be strong enough to achieve her goal.

When divine love thoroughly permeates your subconscious, your innocence is restored. With that purity of heart, you are free to be an open book. You can talk about your own flaws, failures, and mistakes without shame because you recognize that it is through your weaknesses that you are made strong.

The Peace Mind

Whenever we are attacked, our immediate response is either fight or flight. This acute stress reaction is usually triggered when we encounter something either mentally or physically terrifying. Our bodies release hormones to prepare us to stay and deal with a threat or run away from it. In the case of a physical threat, such as a fire in the house or a hungry lion about to attack, the fight-or-flight response can be beneficial. The imminent danger causes our bodies to go into high alert, which gives us that extra adrenaline to find a way to stay alive.

But the psychologically acute mental stress response is not actually rooted in a deadly threat against the body, but an attack on a person's sense of self—their egoic mind. When someone criticizes, attacks, or pressures you, it activates anxiety, worry, and stress. You will either fight back in defense or run away from the conflict. Since each reaction is rooted in fear, it does not lead to inner freedom, nor does it lead to conflict resolution. In fact, it sinks you further into the claws of the ego, which alienates you from unconditional love.

But when you are conscious of divine love, your comeback to criticism and personal attacks is not motivated by a need to defend your sense of self. If you are wrong, then you just apologize. But if you are unjustly charged, then you know that the reason why the other is upset is less about you and more about their own inner conflict. What you said or did triggered fear, aroused insecurity, or provoked guilt in them. The ego in them then pushed back against what they perceived as a threat to their sense of self. Therefore, they attacked you since their fight-or-flight response mechanism was activated.

In some cases, love's response is to not defend yourself, which only inflames both your and the attacker's egos. So when someone sends you a nasty email, disagrees with your post on Facebook, or speaks poorly about you to others, you don't get frazzled and defend yourself or attack them back. Silence is sometimes the best response to people's bitterness and pain.

Yet, at other times, a response is warranted, but not for the sake of winning the argument. Instead, the goal is compassion and healing for the other person. If the conflict can cause the others to pause in self-reflection for a moment, then perhaps they can search out the divine love that's hidden within them. But even if they won't, then you still have maintained awareness of the love that is the core essence of your being. If you are consumed with anger, then it drains your energy, and you needlessly drift away from your focus. Remaining conscious of divine love will, however, keep your heart at peace.

Maybe that's why Jesus did not reply to any of the charges brought against him when standing before Pilate, the Roman prefect, and adjudicator in Judea. Pilate was amazed because it defied everything he, as a judge, had learned about people. Everyone defends themselves, even if they have to lie and betray a friend or ally. But Jesus remained silent when the insults were hurled his way. When Jesus finally spoke with Pilate, the conversation was not in defense, but a prompting for Pilate to look inside himself and find the truth.

A mindset of love defies our logic and runs contrary to every impulse of the ego. Yet, in the end, love always wins. Jesus may have suffered, but he still maintained the peace to accomplish his destiny. The final outcome was a new kind of life. How could there have been any different outcome to love? If love is not the Source of Life, humanity is doomed to destruction and eventual annihilation—life here on earth is then a meaningless wandering in the pursuit of whatever the ego needs to feel special and superior. But when we surrender to love as the ultimate reality of the universe, living as love is our only possible path.

The Nonjudgmental Mind

Of all the conceivable thoughts in the realm of possibility, the mind compulsively gravitates toward negative judgments about ourselves and others. These reactive judgments will often arise out of nowhere and involve virtually anything. Whether we are driving and someone cuts in front of us, a co-worker doesn't perform to our expectation, or we lack time to spend with our children, our thoughts are inclined to form judgments about our own performance, situations that we find ourselves in, or people that we encounter. Even when we meet someone for the first time, we make instant conclusions about that person based on their looks, clothes, gender, race, wealth, job, nationality, fame, or even the jewelry they wear.

The judgments we make, however, convey more about us than them. The ego that seeks to feel special and superior makes a snap verdict about whether that individual will enhance our sense of self. That decision is based on what story—whether heroic, self-pitying, or guilt-ridden—the mind is currently obsessed with. So the judgment of that other person is not really based on facts, but instead on our interpretation of facts. And that opinion is rooted in an unconscious bias to whatever strengthens the ego.

So when you meet an attractive person and they seem interested in you, you feel good about yourself, and therefore you make a favorable judgment about them. But if that person gives you the cold shoulder, your sense of self is threatened, and therefore you will subconsciously try to find something in that person to criticize and complain about.

Another way we judge people is by placing them in a category and giving them a label. If our primary sense of identity is our occupation, often the first question we ask a person we meet for the first time is: "What do you do?" Their profession is a way for us to subconsciously determine whether the person is inferior or superior to us. Or when we derive our worth and sense of self from our political affiliation, we try to determine whether the person is a conservative or liberal. If his political persuasions oppose ours, we instinctively we feel more enlightened than him, and hence our ego is enhanced.

Whatever prejudicial judgments we make, whether against ourselves or others, it is always rooted in one of the egoic stages of consciousness. The inner nagging silent whisper of *I am not enough for unconditional love* looks for ways to become more deserving of love than others by critically condemning those we consider less than us, or complaining about the ones who make us feel inferior about ourselves. When we meet people who we consider more significant than us, we try to attach ourselves to them to make ourselves more acceptable for love. If they reject or abandon us, we tear them apart as a way to enhance our sense of self and make ourselves deserving of respect in ways that they are not.

This judgmental mind is the cause of so much of our suffering. When we condemn others, we block off unconditional love from flowing freely through us. We become unconscious of divine love because we have made "otherness" our enemy. The truth that Christ is everything has been darkened, and we are unable to perceive our oneness with all things.

But when we awaken to love within us, we gain a nonjudgmental mind that is free of prejudice. Writers of early Christian texts portrayed this nonjudgmental mind as the mind of Christ. Since Christ is everything, there is neither Gentile nor Jew, slave nor free man, male nor female. Everything is Christ, so if I condemn another, I'm actually condemning Christ and myself as Christ. But when I'm enlightened to Christ in me, my thoughts about myself and others have been purified by unconditional love. Therefore, as you become more attuned to divine love within you, you will embrace your own flaws and the differences between you and other people. You will care less about how other people see you and find commonality with others who differ from you. Since what we judge we punish, you will not punish yourself nor withdraw love for others. Forgiveness, patience, and kindness will effortlessly flow through you, healing your heart and warmly touching the world around you.

And Now to the Story of the Muslim Premier...

For more than two decades, I had the opportunity to be the main speaker at large city festivals internationally. During the early part of this millennium, I was invited to speak in an area where about half the population was Christian and other half was Muslim, including the provincial Premier. Since our events attract tens of thousands of people, it is not uncommon for politicians to attend the opening of the festival, and this time was no different.

As I arrived to speak on opening night, I was told that I had to wait until the Premier came. Twenty minutes ticked by. I checked my watch again, and a half hour had passed. I became increasingly annoyed at what I assumed to be political grandstanding. Finally, the Premier arrived. He seemed to relish the reception he received from the large crowd, taking his time to address the people. When the time finally came for me to speak, I was agitated. There was barely any time left, so I made some backhanded comments that I knew the crowd would not pick up on, but that would let the Premier know that I was not pleased with his political speechmaking made at my expense. The tension between us was palpable. Although nothing was said in front of the people, I knew that my introduction to this man had not been a positive encounter.

The following day, I realized that the barrier between us had no chance of dissolving if I maintained my judgmental attitude, which I realized much later was a throwback to my old egoic mindset of seeing through the lens of duality, or the knowledge of good and evil.

So I asked Elias Shija, my national festival director, if he could arrange a meeting with the Premier. Elias tried his best, but we had a long wait without any response. We needed another approach: visiting the Premier's office buildings. However, official after official told us that the Premier was unable to speak with us. It was then that I remembered that the nation's Vice President had died that same week, and the country was in official mourning. Many citizens of the nation were stopping by the government building signing their names and making a donation as a symbol of respect. So I decided that I would also make a sizeable donation in honor of the Vice President at the office of the Premier.

A few moments later, I was told the Premier would see us for a brief moment. As we entered the office, his staff was courteous, but the tension from the night before was still there. Looking at the Premier, I knew from his stern face that he had not appreciated our earlier meeting. Before he had a chance to speak, I reached out my hand and looked into his eyes. I expressed my condolences for the passing of the Vice President, and then took the next few minutes to speak words of honor toward him.

As I continued to speak positive, affirming words, I noticed that his countenance changed. When I finished speaking, the Premier thanked me for coming to help people in his province. Soon we parted ways again, this time in peace. He told me that I was more than welcome to his region at any time.

When we awaken to divine love within us, we shift from an egoic consciousness that seeks to protect and defend its own reality about what is good and evil, right or wrong. Trying to win an argument with the Premier about who was right was meaningless. Instead, being conscious of divine love somehow compelled me to act contrary to the impulses of the ego, and display an attitude of graciousness, generosity, and kindness.

Judgmental attitudes and hypocritical actions tear us apart, but the attitude and words that reveal selfless divine love bring healing, restoration, and wholeness between people, families, and nations. This is what happens when you awaken to your *true self*. A new person emerges. You are being transformed by love to be love.

14

A BETTER WORLD

Awakening to our *true self* gives us confidence in the inherent power of love. We can once again imagine a world where no one goes hungry, and everyone has the means to provide for themselves and their families.

We can picture a planet where injustice and inequality are wiped out and every life has dignity and value. We can envision environmental protection, political liberty, an end to discrimination and persecution, protection against crime and violence, affordable and nutritious food, better health care, and good education for everyone. We can dream of a world where everyone enjoys peace and prosperity.

Yet, when we look at the challenges facing the world, it's not difficult to become disillusioned. From large-scale conflicts, mass shootings, horrible acts of murder, discrimination based on race and gender, poverty, government corruption, climate change, lack of education, and lack of economic opportunities, we are faced with issues that appear unsolvable. While speaking with a former CIA agent who had been stationed in Europe, I was struck by his pessimism about the world. With all the efforts being made for global stability, justice, and equality, he still glumly concluded that there is no chance of peace in the world for the next 1,000 years.

So is there a path out of our collective insanity?

Can the story of humanity turn into a narrative where love wins?

If so, how can we participate in creating a better world?

Let's explore three basic core principles that will improve life on our magnificent planet: living with purpose, finding your mission, and serving the underprivileged.

Live With Purpose

Within every person, there's a longing for meaning in life. We want our human experience to matter. At some point, therefore, most of us are faced with the question of purpose. Why am I here? What's the real meaning of life?

We often assume that what we do is our purpose. But *doing* is a *function*. That function varies throughout our human experience. Our role within a family structure evolves. Our careers change, and our goals and dreams fluctuate. The endeavors we pursue and the work we engage in are essential to what it means to be human. Yet what we do is not our primary purpose.

Instead, our purpose is to find our *true self* within and to manifest our spirit's oneness with God through our human experience. Awakening to this Christ-centric consciousness is the same for every human being, and it's what gives meaning to life. When you are aware of Christ in you, and you see Christ in everything and identify with everything as Christ, the objective for your human existence is revealed. Experiencing this reality is merely to be *present* with whatever is *now*. It's being conscious of the divine *presence* resting in all things.

Being aware of your *true self* then guides what you do. Your function is meaningful and even essential. But the role you play by doing is secondary to your purpose. Some careers may last for decades. Other tasks may only be momentary. Yet what you are *doing* is never a substitute for *being*. So in whatever you do—whether it's selling real estate, helping your kids with their homework, or attending a job improvement workshop—be mindful of your oneness with the SOURCE OF LIFE and bring that awareness into every moment of your *doing*.

One way to practice bringing your *true self* into all of your endeavors is to pause throughout the day for 30-60 seconds and become completely still and aware of the divine *presence* in everything. Sometimes this involves closing your eyes and focusing inwardly, which helps you become aware of the *presence of love* in you. Other times, it could mean stepping outside your office or home in complete silence to notice without judgment the intrinsic spirit of a flower, a tree, a bird, or another human being.

Before I speak at any event, connect with someone on the phone, or sit down to write, I often become entirely still. Even if it's only for 10 seconds, my thoughts yield to an awareness of the divine *presence* in all things—the people and the projects that are present in the moment. Out of that awareness flows calm and confident wisdom for what I'm engaged in. And when things are not working out the way I hoped, and emotions seek to distract me, I'm able to return to that place of awareness within me and find comfort, peace, and happiness.

So living a purpose-driven life that creates a better world is more than finding the mysterious "right" thing to do or some grandiose mission to accomplish. It requires nothing more than remaining in a state of consciousness of your *true self* and manifesting that awareness by being completely present in every moment. It's simple, but it's not always easy.

As more of us experience this awakening, it will impact the collective consciousness of the earth and eventually transform culture and society. This is not so much through sharing our beliefs and mental ideas. Since transformation is an inward awareness beyond your thoughts, it cannot be legislated, imposed, or even taught as a belief. What attracts others is the energy that emanates from you. Your spirit that is one with God radiates love through your presence and through the words you use. When a person is ready to be awakened, your presence and words will then spark something within them that desires the freedom of finding their *true self* within.

Jesus referenced this when he said that the words that I speak are spirit (energy) and they are life (aliveness). The words of Jesus were not neatly packaged doctrinal statements or beliefs to wrap one's head around, but they contained energy that bypassed the mind and touched the *spirit* of the people listening. So life-giving were the presence and words of Jesus that people were healed. Still, Jesus never gave himself credit for the miracles, but always said that it was their faith that had made them whole. Even if it was just momentarily, being with Jesus had awakened them to the dimension in them that was one with God. This was faith because it transported them beyond thoughts, beliefs, and mental constructs into that place of spiritual awareness. Healing was now the most natural outcome.

The path forward, then, is not through converting others to our worldview. Instead, our purpose is to find our own *true self* within. Out of that Christ-centric consciousness, grows the fruits of love, joy, peace, and kindness that can circumvent minds and touch the *spirit* of others. The stories we share, the ideas we exchange, and the beliefs we hold are simply guideposts to find that dimension within us that is *love*.

In June 2006, while in Tanzania for a conference where I was the featured keynote speaker, I had a dream one night that had a profound effect on me. In the dream, I found myself sitting on a chair near the head of a long, gray table. Diagonally across from me and slightly pushed back in disinterest, sat a well-known Hollywood actress. I tried to communicate with her, but we had nothing in common, so our time together consisted of mostly awkward pauses. I thought about how I could share my beliefs with her, but my words were empty, meaningless, and hollow. I barely believed them myself. Then I saw a black silhouette that appeared to be an African child sitting at the head of the table. I stood up and leaned over from behind with my arms around the shoulders of the child, similarly to what I often do with my own children. It was a pure expression of fatherly love. Then I asked the Hollywood actress about her own children, and suddenly we made a connection. We communicated in laughter, and the barrier between us came down.

Out of that exchange based on respect, friendship, and compassion for one another, we were able to share our ideas and thoughts freely. The motivation was not to convert the other to a religious belief, but to help one another experience freedom from the stress, pressure, and emotional pain that is common to everyone.

Although it was just a dream, it communicated an important principle: the path forward for humanity is not through converting others to an intellectual belief system. Such a strategy ultimately becomes just another device of the egoic mindset. Instead, life is found in being present with all things. Awareness of the divine *presence*, in what your senses perceive as *yourself* and *otherness*, is what brings hope to the world. A set of beliefs is never the end-goal, but only ideas to exchange to point us toward finding the Truth in all of us.

Find Your Mission

While everyone shares the same purpose, all of us have unique functions. Our personalities are different, and our talents, abilities, and intelligence vary. So we fill our own individual roles and take on various tasks that match our personal gifting. The purpose is still the same for everyone, but what we do differs. Yet our responsibilities complement one another and contribute to the emergence of the Christ-centric consciousness on earth.

Before we are awakened to our *true self*, our pursuits are generally rooted in the egoic mind. As children, we are encouraged to have dreams about what we want to do, and what kind of career and lifestyle we want. Often expectations are also placed upon us. A parent, grandparent, teacher, clergy, or friend projects onto us an image of what they want us to do. The fear of the egoic mind in them seeks to mold us into doing what they do or doing what they always wanted to do but never did. So we unconsciously follow a career path and make lifestyle choices based on the need for acceptance and approval by the people who have influenced us.

Other times, we pursue a career because the accolades and the honor we get from our work become the artificial acceptance and love that our egoic mind craves. Of course, for many, work merely represents a way to survive or support their lifestyle, but that is also commonly rooted in the egoic mind. Work is something we endure, but we live for our time off. And then when we are not at work, we may complain and gripe about the job, and therefore never really experience the joy of being present in the moment.

When you are awakened to your *true self*, your unique role will naturally emerge from within. The infinite wisdom flows through your spirit and guides your path. Your actual part may not be immediately known, because waking up involves first coming to a place of contentment and gratitude in what is *now*. Your happiness and fulfillment are ultimately not grounded in what you do but in who you are. Once you are at peace with *what is* and rest in the awareness of the *spirit*, an inner knowing (or *calling*) will naturally emerge as inclinations of what to do. This doesn't mean it's a lifetime call. Change is inevitable as we continue to develop and grow in our wisdom.

The *calling* is also not necessarily giving up everything and pursuing a life of solace or working for a charity in an impoverished area. Those are commendable roles that some will be called to. But for most, the mission is a professional career that you *know* you are supposed to engage in. What's important is that your purpose shines through your function. You are guided to do because you are aware of the divine *presence* in you and in everything you encounter. So your mission then is not something that you have to figure out, which is rooted in fear and leads to stress and ultimately more suffering. But when you are aware of the divine *presence* within you, it will at some point, even if it takes some time, show up as an idea to explore or a passion to follow.

As you embark on your career, your happiness and fulfillment are not found in the achievement of your mission, but in living each moment aware of a deep sense of peace and love. For example, as I'm writing this book, the goal is to publish it so that it can serve people as a guide to finding their *true self*. Yet, my sense of satisfaction and enjoyment is not in the goal, but in the actual writing of each word. I'm aware of the divine *presence*, which is my purpose. With every new word that I write, I'm living my purpose. Once the book is done, what I do will change, but my purpose stays the same: to remain in that state of awareness of love, and for that presence to shine through whatever I do. What you do then is never as important as who you are, because your *doing* follows your *being*.

When you are in that place of awareness, you are attuned to the infinite wisdom of God, which gives you the grace to do more than you ever thought possible. Your mind, remodeled by your awakened consciousness, is no longer restricted by the nagging voice of fear. The ego's unconscious storyline of *I'm not enough*, which used to limit your potential, has yielded to the *spirit's* affirmation of *I am love*, thus breaking the limitations that fear produced in your mind.

Science is now discovering that the brain is inherently wired for love and that the egoic mindset puts your mind out of sync with your wired-for-love design, damaging both your brain and body.[1] This mindset of negativity obviously reduces the brain's ability to help you actualize your potential. As David Shenk in *The Genius Inside All of Us* writes, "New science suggests that few of us know our true limits," and adds, "the vast majority of us have not even come close to tapping what scientists call our 'unactualized potential.'"[2]

So if your brain's default setting is to be attuned to love, and fear damages your brain, the obvious conclusion is that being awakened to your *true self* boosts your emotional wellbeing and intelligence, and enhances your ability to innovate. Some of the most creative geniuses in history attribute their inventions to finding it from a place within, beyond their own thoughts.

In due course, awakening to our *true self* where our *doing* derives from our *being*, and where our *being* is one with the infinite presence of the universe, will lead to a better world. The collective unfolding of our *true self* will pave the way to the full manifestation of the divine wisdom (logos) on the earth. Christ-centric consciousness will permeate everything that we do; thus creating a better and more peaceful planet.

Serve the Underprivileged

The wisdom of the egoic mind is a world where power is linked with material wealth and physical strength. The strong survive and succeed, while the weak fail and get left with very little. The ego, therefore, always looks for ways to get ahead.

But love's wisdom is uniquely different. Weakness is actually a strength because it makes us come to the end of the ego and accept unconditional love. This is one reason why the story of Jesus' crucifixion is so compelling to us. Jesus was utterly vulnerable on that cross. The anguish was beyond anything any of us can possibly understand. Yet, we see in Jesus strength in adversity. We find that in the end that love wins, and weakness becomes a strength.

In the global awakening of the Christ-centric consciousness, it would seem to me that this principle holds true not only for each of us individually, but also collectively. Often as individuals, we awaken to our essence of love through suffering because torment makes us more receptive to finding our *true self* within. Likewise, the most vulnerable groups in society are generally more open to experiencing transformation.

For example, the success of Jesus was not in his ability to start a new religion. Being a religious founder was never part of his agenda. But the way of the famous rabbi was to reach out to the ones who were considered less and were rejected by society. By offering compassion and forgiveness to the adulterous woman who, according to the religious tradition, was to be punished by stoning to death, the Nazarene demonstrated how living as love creates a better world. Whether Jesus was eating with the hated tax-collectors, who worked for the hostile government and stole money for personal gain, or extending words of healing to the child of the general of the occupying military force, the masterful teacher exemplified how the awakened life always brings hope to whatever society and religion oppose.

Once, when a large crowd was clamoring for Jesus, parents with infants came to him. But since the followers of Jesus considered the little children to be less than the adults, they pushed them away. However, Jesus stopped them and said, let the children come unto me. Unless you become like them, you shall not enter the kingdom of God, Jesus continued. What Jesus suggested here was that the defenseless are most receptive to unconditional love because they are less entrapped by the ego.

In the same manner, like Jesus, we are beacons of light of unconditional love to the most vulnerable among us. When we awaken to our *true self*, we identify with the sufferings of others and extend compassion to them. Love is who we are. Therefore, love is what we do. And love is unveiled where there's suffering.

I began my work with orphaned children in Tanzania about a year after I had my transformative encounter with divine love in 2006. Working with children, or being involved with humanitarian work, had never been on my list of life goals. But after my dream on June 30, 2006, I was moved with compassion for AIDS orphans in Africa. At the time, I didn't know what to do. But later that year, I went with a team, including my friend Daniel Kooman, a young filmmaker, to film a documentary called *Africa Sing Me Your Song*.

After meeting a lot of officials, I told the team that we needed to find some orphaned children for the film. While standing on the street, two young boys, Juma and Haruna, came up to us begging for money. Both the children were covered in dust, with no shoes on their feet, and they wore ripped t-shirts and filthy shorts. After giving them some clothes and feeding them, we asked where they lived. They took us to a place behind a bar, where at some point, someone had intended to build a house. All that had been constructed were stone walls about two feet high. There was no roof, and the floor was a mixture of cement and a patch of grass littered with broken beer bottles thrown there by people at the bar.

At the time, we didn't know what to do. But a few months later, Daniel and I flew back, along with my son, Nathanael, in search of the two boys. By that time, they had moved. But after a few hours, we finally found them. They were living with 5 other orphaned children in a small hut about 6 feet by 6 feet. That day, I promised them that they would never have to beg again. Several months later, we were able to raise enough funds to build all the children a new home in one of the most beautiful neighborhoods in Tabora, Tanzania, where they still live.

Since then, we have helped hundreds of other children in that region. We also started a charity called Juma's World that works in impoverished villages to better the lives of the most vulnerable in the world. Before my experience with unconditional love during intense physical pain at the beginning of 2006, my interest in helping the most vulnerable among us was virtually non-existent, except for the occasional donation to ease my conscience or to enhance my ego when others were watching. But when I was transformed by love, something shifted inside of me and serving the needs of others became an effortless instinct.

My experience is not unique. Sitting down with you, I know you could share how awakening to your core essence of love has made you more generous and compassionate toward the ones considered less valuable by society. Because finding your *true self* transforms not only yourself but the way you perceive and treat others.

As you identify with the humanity in others, the line between *what is in here* and *what is out there* becomes indistinct. In truth, the oneness you share with others is what keeps you most aware of the presence of *Love* within you. You have found your *true self—I am love*—not just in yourself, but in everyone and everything. You have awakened to who you are. *You are Love!*

REFERENCES AND RECOMMENDATIONS

After my healing from cluster headaches in 2006, I would go for hikes almost every day, reflecting upon what I was feeling inside. Everything I knew was crumbling around me, including my religious beliefs. Yet, it was during these hikes that I became increasingly more aware of a *presence* within me that permeated with love. At first, I didn't know how to put into words what I was experiencing. But the more I spent time in contemplation, the more my spiritual understanding was transformed.

During those early days of going for extended hikes, I naively did not know if anyone had ever experienced what was happening to me. Neither did I know of any books written about what I was feeling and thinking. Slowly, I discovered that throughout history, spiritual mystics, philosophers, and thinkers from almost every background had not only had their own transformative experiences, but volumes of books had been written with extraordinary depths of insight about a mystical and outside-the-box spirituality. I also began to take an interest in science, and specifically in quantum physics, and realized that science and spirituality was not opposing forces, but intermingled successfully.

I can no longer remember all the books and voices that have helped me put words to my experience and shaped my writings. But I have included a list of books and authors (in no specific order) that I can still recall that have inspired me and influenced my writings.

Anything by the following authors:

- Thomas Merton
- Pierre Teilhard de Chardin
- Rumi
- Meister Eckhart
- Richard Rohr
- Eckhart Tolle
- Rob Bell
- Peter Enns

Specific books that have inspired me:

- *The Unbearable Wholeness of Being* - Ilio Delio
- *Biocentrism* - Robert Lanza
- *Echo of the Soul* – J. Philip Newell
- *A Brief History of Everything* – Ken Wilber
- *How God Changes Your Brain* – Andrew Newberg
- *Switch On Your Brain* - Dr. Caroline Leaf
- *The Wisdom of Jesus* - Cynthia Bourgeault.
- *The Mastery of Love* - Don Miguel Ruiz (I read this book several times; it's that good)
- *A Return To Love* – Marrianne Williamson
- *Man's Search For Meaning* – Victor E. Frankl

- *The Fourth Dimension* - David Yonggi Cho
- *Wired for Success, Programmed for Failure* - Dr. James B. Richards
- *The Healing Gospels* - Derek Flood
- *A Course in Miracles* – (Helen Schucman)
- *Taking the Quantum Leap* – Fred A. Wolf

NOTES

1. The Search for Freedom

1. www.apa.org/monitor/2017/05/alternative-facts
2. www.apa.org/monitor/2017/05/alternative-facts

2. What Is Love?

1. Pierre Teilhard de Chardin, Human Energy, (New York: Harcourt Brace Jovanovich, 199), 72
2. Daniel C. Matt, God, and the Big Bang: Discovering Harmony Between Science and Spirituality (Woodstock, VT: Jewish Literature Publishing, 2001
3. Fritjof Capra, The Tao of Physics, 4th ed., (Shambala Publications)

3. Stages of Consciousness

1. Acts of the Apostles, Chapter 17 (The Bible)*
2. The Epistle of Ephesians, Chapter 4 (The Bible)*
3. The Epistle of Colossians, Chapter 3 (The Bible)*
4. The Epistle of Colossians, Chapter 1 (The Bible)*

7. The Myth of Failure

1. The 1st Epistle of John, Chapter 4 (The Bible)*
2. www.cac.org/the-meaning-of-spiritual-love-2018-11-07/

8. The Wonder of Who You Are

1. Bob Berman, Robert Lanza, Biocentrism: How Life and Consciousness are the Keys to Understanding the True Nature of the Universe, Benbella Books, Inc.
2. www.content.time.com/subscriber/article/0,33009,2119322-2,00.html
3. Bob Berman, Robert Lanza, Biocentrism: How Life and Consciousness are the Keys to Understanding the True Nature of the Universe, Benbella Books, Inc.
4. Bob Berman, Robert Lanza, Biocentrism: How Life and Consciousness are the Keys to Understanding the True Nature of the Universe, Benbella Books, Inc.

9. The Unfolding Creation

1. Teilhard de Chardin, P., The Phenomenon of Man, William Collins Sons & Co. Ltd, London, 1980
2. The Epistle of Colossians, Chapter 3, (The Bible)*

10. The Heart Transformation

1. Proverbs of Solomon, Chapter 23 (The Bible)*
2. Proverbs of Solomon, Chapter 4 (The Bible)*
3. Proverbs of Solomon, Chapter 14 (The Bible)*
4. Proverbs of Solomon, Chapter 17 (The Bible)*

11. When Faith Reveals Who You Are

1. Hebrews, Chapter 11, (The Bible)*
2. Hebrews, Chapter 12, (The Bible)*
3. Hebrews, Chapter 12, (The Bible)*

13. A Mindset of Love

1. www.ncbi.nlm.nih.gov/pmc/articles/PMC3485650

14. A Better World

1. Robert Weinhold, "Epigenetics: The Science of Change," Environmental Perspectives (March 2006)
2. David Shenk, The Genius in All of Us: New Insights into Genetics, Talent, and IQ, Anchor

ABOUT DAVID YOUNGREN

David Youngren is a philanthropist, author, and an international teacher (has spoken to more than one million people at live events), who inspires and guides spiritual seekers from every background to awaken to their true self.

Youngren – formerly a Canadian evangelical pastor, Bible College President, and a crusade and TV evangelist – had a profound inner experience of unconditional love in 2006 that transformed his life and left him questioning his religious beliefs. Disillusioned by religious tribalism, David began to find beauty and truth in all traditions and religions, even if they were not his own.

David spearheads several international initiatives, including Way of Love Community and Juma's World. He lives with his family in southern California.

Made in the USA
Columbia, SC
17 October 2020